The First World War

A Brief History with Documents

D0061654

Related Titles in
THE BEDFORD SERIES IN HISTORY AND CULTURE
Advisory Editors: Lynn Hunt, *University of California, Los Angeles*
David W. Blight, *Yale University*
Bonnie G. Smith, *Rutgers University*
Natalie Zemon Davis, *University of Toronto*

Napoleonic Foot Soldiers and Civilians: A Brief History with Documents
Rafe Blaufarb, *Florida State University,* and Claudia Liebeskind,
Florida State University

Lenin and the Making of the Soviet State: A Brief History with Documents
Jeffrey Brooks, *Johns Hopkins University,* and Georgiy Chernyavskiy,
Ukrainian Academy of Culture

July 1914: Soldiers, Statesmen, and the Coming of the Great War: A Brief Documentary History
Samuel R. Williamson, Jr., *University of the South,* and Russel Van Wyk,
University of North Carolina at Chapel Hill

The Nazi State and German Society: A Brief History with Documents
Robert G. Moeller, *University of California, Irvine*

Pearl Harbor and the Coming of the Pacific War: A Brief History with Documents and Essays
Akira Iriye, *Harvard University*

Pioneers of European Integration and Peace, 1945–1963: A Brief History with Documents
Sherrill Brown Wells, *George Washington University*

THE BEDFORD SERIES IN HISTORY AND CULTURE

The First World War

A Brief History with Documents

Susan R. Grayzel

University of Mississippi

BEDFORD / ST. MARTIN'S   Boston ◆ New York

For Bedford/St. Martin's

Publisher for History: Mary V. Dougherty
Executive Editor for History: Traci M. Crowell
Director of Development for History: Jane Knetzger
Senior Editor: Heidi L. Hood
Developmental Editor: Ann Kirby-Payne
Associate Editor: Jennifer Jovin
Editorial Assistant: Laura Kintz
Executive Marketing Manager: Jenna Bookin Barry
Production Supervisor: Victoria Sharoyan
Project Management: Books By Design, Inc.
Cartography: Mapping Specialists, Ltd.
Permissions Manager: Kalina K. Ingham
Text Design: Claire Seng-Niemoeller
Cover Design: Andrea M. Corbin and Marine Miller
Cover Photo: Women in the First World War, Ministry of Information First World War
    Official Collection. D. McLellan, photographer. Courtesy of the Imperial War
    Museum.
Composition: Achorn International, Inc.
Printing and Binding: RR Donnelley and Sons

President, Bedford/St. Martin's: Denise B. Wydra
Presidents, Macmillan Higher Education: Joan E. Feinberg and Tom Scotty
Director of Marketing: Karen R. Soeltz
Director of Production: Susan W. Brown
Associate Production Director: Elise S. Kaiser
Manager, Publishing Services: Andrea Cava

Library of Congress Control Number: 2012939217

Manufactured in the United States of America.

7   6   5   4   3   2
f   e   d   c   b   a

For information, write: Bedford / St. Martin's, 75 Arlington Street, Boston, MA 02116
(617-399-4000)

ISBN: 978-0-312-45887-4

Acknowledgments

Acknowledgments and copyrights are continued at the back of the book on
pages 171–72, which constitute an extension of the copyright page.

Distributed outside North America by PALGRAVE MACMILLAN
Houndmills, Basingstoke, Hampshire RG21 6XS

Foreword

The Bedford Series in History and Culture is designed so that readers can study the past as historians do.

The historian's first task is finding the evidence. Documents, letters, memoirs, interviews, pictures, movies, novels, or poems can provide facts and clues. Then the historian questions and compares the sources. There is more to do than in a courtroom, for hearsay evidence is welcome, and the historian is usually looking for answers beyond act and motive. Different views of an event may be as important as a single verdict. How a story is told may yield as much information as what it says.

Along the way the historian seeks help from other historians and perhaps from specialists in other disciplines. Finally, it is time to write, to decide on an interpretation and how to arrange the evidence for readers.

Each book in this series contains an important historical document or group of documents, each document a witness from the past and open to interpretation in different ways. The documents are combined with some element of historical narrative — an introduction or a biographical essay, for example — that provides students with an analysis of the primary source material and important background information about the world in which it was produced.

Each book in the series focuses on a specific topic within a specific historical period. Each provides a basis for lively thought and discussion about several aspects of the topic and the historian's role. Each is short enough (and inexpensive enough) to be a reasonable one-week assignment in a college course. Whether as classroom or personal reading, each book in the series provides firsthand experience of the challenge — and fun — of discovering, recreating, and interpreting the past.

Lynn Hunt
David W. Blight
Bonnie G. Smith
Natalie Zemon Davis

for Bedford and provided many valuable critiques of earlier drafts: D. R. Dorondo, Western Carolina University; Martha Hanna, University of Colorado at Boulder; Susan Kent, University of Colorado at Boulder; Brock Millman, University of Western Ontario; John H. Morrow Jr., University of Georgia; George Robb, William Paterson University; Lynn L. Sharp, Whitman College; Tyler Stovall, University of California, Berkeley; Paul Werth, University of Nevada, Las Vegas; and Jay Winter, Yale University.

Closer to home, I appreciate the questions posed by undergraduate and graduate students at the University of Mississippi who have taken my classes on the First World War and on modern Europe and its colonial empires. Above all, I am thankful for the close readings, insights, and boundless support of Joe Ward. I greatly appreciate the willingness of my daughters—Sarah, Rebecca, and Miranda—to tolerate my hours in the study and to provide welcome distractions from all my books on death and destruction. Finally, I lovingly dedicate this book to my father, Arthur I. Grayzel, a physician with a scholarly mind who has exhibited an endless joie de vivre as he has waged his own war against disease.

Susan R. Grayzel

of this book. Several of them appear here for the first time in English. They come from men and women, combatants and noncombatants, Europeans and non-Europeans, and they illustrate both the historical events that defined the conflict and how people who lived during the war years reflected on its meaning at the time. Treaties, agreements, news items, and diplomatic dispatches are presented alongside intimate diary entries, letters, essays, poems, and prose to give students an opportunity to explore the far-reaching effects of the Great War.

Clearly, no one volume can do justice to the sheer breadth of the lived experiences of this conflict or to all of its motivations and consequences. Inevitably, the greatest focus here is on the major European participant states. To make comparisons of varying wartime experiences along national lines easier, some of the documents within each section are arranged so that they illustrate a variety of perspectives on the war from different countries, genders, and social groups.

The documents and introduction are further supported with tools to help students firmly grasp the events of the war and many of their meanings. A selection of maps in the introduction will enable students to visualize both the main settings and the global scale of the war, and a chronology at the end of the book outlines important events. The questions for consideration invite further discussion, and a selected bibliography offers opportunities for more in-depth exploration.

ACKNOWLEDGMENTS

This book began when Lynn Hunt invited me to take on this daunting project several years ago. It proved far more challenging than I could have imagined then, but I am nonetheless glad that I agreed and remain grateful to her for her belief in the necessity of such a volume. Most especially, I am indebted to the staff at Bedford/St. Martin's, especially Heidi Hood and freelance editor Ann Kirby-Payne, for all their help and patience as I tried to condense sprawling and contentious debates into the confines of this series, and to Jennifer Jovin and Laura Kintz for providing essential editorial support. Thanks also to Andrea Cava at Bedford and Nancy Benjamin of Books By Design for guiding the book through production, and to copyeditor Barbara Jatkola. I also want to acknowledge my many fellow historians of the First World War, particularly members of the International Society for First World War Studies online community (a treasure trove of information about the Great War). I am indebted to the following colleagues, who reviewed the manuscript

Preface

The First World War has long been viewed as a decisive turning point in European and world history, and over the past thirty years, scholarship on the war has expanded greatly, deepening our understanding of its origins, course, and consequences. Yet although the literature about the war has thus broadened, some of the materials for teaching its history do not yet encompass the most recent historiography. This volume offers an introductory essay and a range of primary source materials—both widely known and more obscure—that will facilitate an appreciation of the war itself, as well as its causes and outcomes. It aims to familiarize students with various perspectives on the war that emphasize its roots in nineteenth-century nationalism, imperialism, and militarism; the emergence of a new and modern kind of "total war"; and the war as a cultural phenomenon.

Traditionally, scholars have treated the origins and aftermath of World War I as subjects separate from the war itself. This volume, in contrast, integrates them into both the introduction and the documents. Part one, the introduction, is divided into three sections. The first section provides a snapshot of Europe in the years before the war, detailing not only the war's immediate origins (the rise of Europe's "armed camps" and the "alliance system" of the early twentieth century) but also the cultural, social, and political developments of nineteenth- and early-twentieth-century Europe that fostered an atmosphere conducive to the outbreak of war in 1914. The second section places the European experiences of the war in a global context, detailing key events and their effects on those who lived through them. As the introduction's largest section, it covers the full chronological, and much of the global, range of the war. Finally, the third section explores the immediate consequences of the war, addressing not only the treaties that brought the fighting to an end and redrew the map of Europe and beyond, but also some of the social and cultural responses to this conflict.

Each of the introduction's three sections is supported by a corresponding set of documents in part two; these documents are the core

Contents

Noncombatant Voices from the War's Other Fronts

Reflections on the Meaning and Effects of the War

Maps and Illustrations

THE BEDFORD SERIES IN HISTORY AND CULTURE

The First World War

A Brief History with Documents

PART ONE

Introduction:
The First World War and the
Making of a Modern,
Global Conflict

Some events are truly earth-shattering. The First World War was such an occasion—a war so destructive and so seemingly unprecedented that, at the time, it seemed to defy traditional description and became known as "the Great War." From 1914 to 1918, a war that began in Europe raged across this continent and far beyond, involving imperial outposts in Africa and independent states in Asia, as well as populations from both of these areas as well the Americas, Australia, and New Zealand. By the war's end, it had destroyed millions of lives and ravaged the countries in which it took place. A list of the participants tells us a great deal. It includes states that the war helped to destroy, such as tsarist Russia, the dual monarchy of Austria-Hungary, imperial Germany, and the Ottoman Empire. It also takes in nations such as the United States and Japan, which the war helped to solidify as global powers.

Despite claims in the war's later phases that it might be, in the words of novelist H. G. Wells, the "war to end war," in the end World War I's enormous costs and challenges helped reshape warfare, politics, society, and culture in ways that reverberated throughout other twentieth-century conflicts and into the present day. The First World War left both literal and figurative scars on the bodies and lands of its participants, and if we want to understand the modern world that it bequeathed to us, we need to grapple with its origins, experiences, and legacies through primary sources: the words and images of those who lived through this momentous time.

In the Russian poet Anna Akhmatova's "July 1914" (Document 8), the image of fields "warmly watered" by blood hauntingly evokes the costs of the war from its very beginning. If we then move forward to the war's end and look at the *Times* of London's casualty list (Document 41), we can begin to count the dead. The numbers are truly shocking, with losses in the millions. But the list could go on, for there were deaths and injuries that are rarely accounted for in such tallies: from war wounds, such as lungs wrecked by chemical weapons and minds shattered by combat; from diseases made more lethal by malnutrition; and from lives cut short by grief.

In the face of the First World War's death tolls, economic expenditures, social dislocations, political upheavals, and physical and psychological damages, the war can easily seem like only a predictable and tragic mistake. And voices like that of Ahkmatova suggest that some anticipated this as early as 1914. Yet when the war broke out in the summer of that year, it was the culmination of a variety of long- and short-term factors that predisposed leaders of many of the major powers, and some of their constituents, to accept war as the only mechanism by which to resolve their differences.

Why did such a large-scale war occur in 1914? There are multiple and sometimes contradictory explanations. For some postwar commentators, the war demonstrated the collapse of Western civilization, and its origins lay in the West's decline. Others placed the blame on the failures of certain dominant Western political and social movements, so that above all, the war signaled the decline of liberalism—belief in government based on the rights and sovereignty of individuals. For others, the roots can be traced to a combination of specific nineteenth- and twentieth-century political, economic, diplomatic, and military developments. Still others have insisted on the primacy of the ideological triumvirate of nationalism, imperialism, and militarism, which, in combination with a growing belief in Social Darwinism, created a cultural climate in which key segments of the European population were predisposed to accept war when it arrived. Given the complexity, and in some cases the ferocity, of the debates over why what started out as the third Balkan war in as many years evolved so rapidly into a truly global conflict, it is worth examining all of these factors. No simple explanation will suffice, and it is crucial to remind ourselves that even as we seek to make the war's outbreak intelligible, the conflict itself should not be seen as simply inevitable.

THE ORIGINS OF THE FIRST WORLD WAR

Forty years before the start of World War I, the shape of Europe and, as a result, the globe was being altered. New nation-states in central and southern Europe came into being, changing the dynamics of political power on the continent. Nationalism—the notion of belonging to an "imagined community" that could compel loyalty to a geographic entity larger than a locality, to the leaders of this larger nation, and to the symbols that embodied it (a flag, an anthem, a uniform)—grew throughout the nineteenth century.[1] The creation of national armies based on mass conscription took men out of their communities and trained them to fight for an entity that often brought deeply divided populations with local and regional loyalties together to shape them into one nation. Starting in the middle of the nineteenth century, the process of German and Italian unification demonstrated the force of nationalism. While seeking to forge a united Italy, Giuseppe Mazzini—the inspirational architect of Italian nationalism—called on members of disparate communities on the Italian peninsula to love one another as "brothers."[2] In creating the German empire, German nationalists evoked the idea of the *volk* (the folk or people), a group identity rooted in bloodlines and sharing a common ethnic heritage.[3] First manifest as beliefs, then as political movements, nationalism reshaped the terrain of Europe. By 1871, Germany and Italy had emerged as new states, and in the following decades imperial Germany, due to its size and economic success, became a potent force on the continent.

Unsurprisingly, new and old nations competed not only for territory and wealth but also for military supremacy. The subsequent buildup of arms and military forces both reflected and exacerbated national tensions. Warfare also became increasingly industrialized as firepower, accuracy of weapons, and communication improved. The amount of per capita spending on the military climbed in every major European power between 1890 and 1914, and the size of most conscript armies in states that required all men to perform military service for a period of their young adulthood grew as well. All of this contributed to the outbreak of the Great War.[4]

The relatively short duration of conflicts, such as the Crimean War (1853–1856) and Franco-Austrian War (1859), that the major powers had engaged in during the fifty years prior to 1914 was another important factor. Prussia had easily (and quickly) defeated such rivals as Austria, Denmark, and France as it secured territory to establish Germany. The Russo-Japanese War (1904–1905) — a conflict over imperial ambitions in China and Korea that Japan quickly won — offered a striking example of the potential for established European powers such as Russia to be eclipsed by rising states. In conjunction with technological advances, such conflicts seemed to promise short and relatively simple victories in future wars.

However, other wars in far-flung imperial settings, such as the Boer War in southern Africa, also known as the South African War (1899–1902), offered more complicated lessons about international warfare. Developing from an initial conflict in the early 1880s, this war saw the British fighting colonial Dutch settlers, known as Boers, for political control of territory and access to gold mines in the Transvaal, an area under Boer control. Despite having a huge numerical advantage, the British did not achieve an easy victory and defeated the Boers only after facing down a guerrilla war in 1902. This conflict also revealed the extent to which Europeans were willing to use ruthless tactics against imperial opponents, such as the British removing the wives and children of their Boer adversaries from their homes and placing them in camps, where many died. Imperial powers had often treated civilians brutally in colonial conflicts, but the mistreatment of a white settler population provoked an international outcry.[5]

Efforts to promote the glory of the nation-state led in turn to an intensification of imperial entanglements. Competition for control over territory in Africa and Asia heightened national rivalries among European powers. The Berlin Conference in 1884–1885 had set rules to try to manage the colonization of Africa, including the need for states to have full (rather than theoretical) and direct control of the land. These rules resulted in the "scramble for Africa," as European powers tried to claim territory on the continent before rival states could. Most imperial wars of this period involved clashes between colonial subjects and their European rulers, and in the decades before 1914, some colonized subjects agitated to be rid of their imperial masters altogether.

Throughout the late nineteenth and into the early twentieth centuries, the possession of colonial territories provided a source of conflict between competing European states. Although Britain emerged victorious at the end of the Boer War in 1902, it did so at considerable and unexpected material and financial cost. One result was rising British antagonism toward Germany, which it viewed as the main international supporter of the Boers. European colonial empires served as the settings for such conflict and also provided men and materiel with which to wage war in Europe itself. By the end of the first decade of the twentieth century, military officers such as French lieutenant colonel Charles Mangin were extolling the benefits to both France and its African colonial subjects of incorporating African men into the French military (Document 6).[6]

Both nationalism and imperialism drew upon the concept of Social Darwinism, a problematic adaptation of evolutionary theory rooted in the belief that incessant competition among men, "races," and nations was inevitable, that some humans were more "fit" to survive and rule, and that the suffering of the "unfit" was thus nothing that society could remedy. These ideas were loosely inspired by Charles Darwin's theory of the origin of species by natural selection, and proponents claimed them to be "scientific," and thus verifiably true. As a result, they proved especially useful in bolstering ideas about European superiority to indigenous inhabitants of Asia and Africa, and the conflation of "nation" and "race" became pronounced. Some late-nineteenth-century Europeans spoke of potential conflicts between the Anglo-Saxon and Teutonic races (or British and German nations), pronounced the "natural" inferiority of certain populations such as the Slavs (from Poles to Serbs), and encouraged the spread of casual and political anti-Semitism that fueled popular notions of European Jews as irredeemably separate from their nation-states. Perhaps the height of late-nineteenth-century anti-Semitism was marked both by devastating pogroms (organized massacres of Jews) across Russia and by France's Dreyfus affair, in which a high-ranking Jewish member of the French army was falsely accused of treason. The resulting French scandal led to public calls to strip Jews of their citizenship. Among several groups, a "racial" nationalism, adopting some of the language of social Darwinism, trumped the often more liberal and inclusive versions of civic nationalism, and its growth coincided with beliefs in a struggle for the "survival of the fittest" among nations and empires. Such views could help sustain beliefs in the civilizing influence of war.

Nationalism and anxiety about international competition also fostered the growth of multinational treaties and alliances that increasingly grouped European states into competing blocks. This alliance system, coupled with the growing significance of militarism, gave rise to a Europe of two "armed camps" in the decades leading up to the First World War. The impetus for the alliance system began in Germany, as its powerful chancellor Otto von Bismarck wanted to isolate France and to avoid war.

Thus the initial aim was to pursue the Three Emperors' League, uniting Germany, Austria-Hungary, and Russia. In the end, the Dual Alliance between Germany and Austria-Hungary that emerged in 1879 reflected these monarchies' desire for a bulwark against Russia (Document 1). When Italy, frustrated by its colonial failures and seeing France as its main imperial rival, joined Germany and Austria-Hungary, the group of three formed the Triple Alliance in 1882. A renewed attempt at a Three Emperors' League lasting from 1881 to 1887 floundered because of tension between Russia and Austria-Hungary. When Kaiser Wilhelm II ascended the German throne in 1888, his own nationalist ambitions led him to foster closer ties with Austria-Hungary and to reject associations with what he regarded as the inferior Slavs, including the Russians.

These interactions did not go unnoticed by Germany's main rival, France. In the 1890s, the French state pursued closer ties with Russia. The French government also sought to resolve its colonial conflicts with Britain in areas such as the Sudan by entering into secret arrangements with the United Kingdom. A 1904 agreement to respect each other's claims to territory in Egypt (conceded to British control) and Morocco (left to France) helped forge the Entente Cordiale (literally, "friendly agreement," implying a diplomatic relationship that fell short of a military alliance). In the face of threats to imperial holdings, ties between these states strengthened, producing by 1907 a Franco-Russian alliance and Anglo-French and Anglo-Russian ententes (understandings or agreements); the last of these became possible only after Russia and Britain were able to resolve their long-standing differences. Various diplomatic associations now linked France, Britain, and Russia together in an arrangement known as the Triple Entente.

Nationalism and militarism in the face of the declining power of the Ottoman Empire further helped create the circumstances that brought international conflict closer to European soil. The Balkan Peninsula—where the Russian, Austro-Hungarian, and Ottoman empires competed for both territory (in some cases) and influence (in all)—erupted into a series of wars in the years immediately preceding 1914. Austria-Hungary's decision in 1908 to annex the territories of Bosnia and Herzegovina (formerly part of the Ottoman Empire, though administered by Austria-Hungary after 1882) aimed to stop the nationalist ambitions of Serbia. Opposition to this move from Russia, the patron of other Slavic states including Serbia, intensified tensions throughout the Balkans. The failing Ottoman Empire then attempted to form an alliance with a more powerful state, quietly approaching first Britain and then Germany. The Ottomans stepped up their efforts when they saw Russia backing their rivals—for example, the Serbs—for power in the Balkans and elsewhere and felt the need for a strong state to help safeguard their territory.[7] When the Young Turks, a group of nationalist reformers, overthrew the sultan in 1908, they searched for (but did not initially find) an ally to bolster their own imperial ambitions against a variety of powers in Europe that saw in the faltering Ottoman regime an opportunity for territorial expansion in North Africa as well as the Balkans.[8] The result of all these strategic arrangements was a Europe more invested in specific alliances than in the notion of the "concert of Europe" that had seemingly prevailed since the conclusion of the Congress of Vienna in 1815.

Crucially, a number of international incidents in the decade between 1904 and 1914 presaged the outbreak of full-scale war. Some of these took place outside Europe, others on the Balkan Peninsula. The cumulative effect of these crises was to strengthen some of the alliances among European states, to disrupt the balance of power, and to provide the immediate justification for mobilizing for war in 1914.

Japan's defeat of Russia in 1905 had a number of consequences. It gave notice to Europeans that their imperial holdings in Asia could come under threat, and in Russia it contributed to the climate that sparked revolution. The Russian Revolution of 1905 forced the most autocratic monarchy in Europe to create a legislative body, however weak its powers, for the first time. This also served as a potent reminder that violence between groups within national borders could potentially topple regimes and states. Russia's defeat by Japan prompted Germany's leaders to test French imperial power in Morocco; the resulting First Moroccan Crisis (1905) ended with an international conference that, to Germany's frustration, confirmed French control in that region. The incident also brought French and British international interests closer together.

When France consolidated its control of Morocco in 1911, the Second Moroccan Crisis occurred. This time, a German gunboat threatened the port of Agadir, and the German government demanded concessions from France. This aggressive use of German naval power ratcheted up fears about Germany's imperial ambitions and somewhat increased support for militarism in both Britain and France. In the end, France gave Germany considerable territory in the French Congo in order to guarantee France's stake in Morocco. Following the events in Morocco, Italy demanded Tripoli from the Ottoman Empire, a move that led to the Turco-Italian War (1911–1912). After a year of fighting, Italy annexed Tripoli, and the Treaty of Lausanne (1912) affirmed Italy's increased imperial holdings and confirmed the glaring political and military weakness of the Ottoman regime.

Italy's victory over the Ottoman Empire also inspired national-ist movements in the Balkans. In particular, it prompted the Balkan League—consisting of Montenegro, Bulgaria, Serbia, and Greece—to declare war on the Ottomans in October 1912. This started the First Balkan War, which ended with a victory for the Balkan states, but the victors could not agree on the spoils. Thus came the Second Balkan War in June 1913. This time, an expansionist Bulgaria lost to Serbia and Greece, aided by Romania and the Ottomans. This war led to the cre-ation of the independent state of Albania, divided Macedonia between Serbia and Greece, and increased the territory of Greece, Romania, and, most significantly, Serbia. Despite the vested interests of Austria-Hungary, Germany, and Russia in the outcome of the war, none of these nations actively intervened, and none of these governments was entirely satisfied by the outcome. Indeed, while Austria-Hungary had thrown its weight behind Bulgaria, Germany had supported the opposition.[9]

Despite these ongoing eruptions of interstate violence, when look-ing back from 1918, some Europeans would refer to the period before World War I as the belle époque, or "beautiful era." Nostalgia infused such perspectives; the era did not seem so beautiful at the time, and not only on account of international conflict. Doubts about the changes wrought by an increasingly industrialized and urbanized society and the growth and energy of socialist parties across Europe plagued conserva-tives, while those in the self-proclaimed avant-garde sought to shock the establishment and push the limits of acceptable behavior. From the perspective of many, decadence, licentiousness, criminality, radical politics (such as anarchism), diminishing borders between classes and the sexes, and new beliefs in the power of irrationality threatened to overturn a relatively stable social and cultural order. In this setting, the Italian thinker F. T. Marinetti—founder of the Futurist movement—and other self-proclaimed critics of nineteenth-century middle-class respect-ability and liberal values saw war as a cathartic good, able to purge a lazy, corrupt European civilization and return it to its heyday.[10] This view is perhaps epitomized by the manifesto issued by the Futurists prior to the outbreak of war praising "danger" and "speed" (Document 5). By 1914, even the renowned German novelist Thomas Mann had determined that war could be "a moral necessity," and German expressionists such as Max Beckmann spoke of how war could bring rejuvenation.[11]

Several treatises and works of imaginative literature anticipated what such a modern global war might look like. As early as the 1890s, writers in Germany, France, and Britain were all producing popular works of fic-tion, some serialized in the mass media, depicting how conflict between these states might occur. Some focused on the political rivalries, while

others, such as British science fiction writer H. G. Wells, focused on how technology and science had potentially changed the nature of war itself. In *The Time Machine* (1895), *The War of the Worlds* (1898), and *The War in the Air* (1908), Wells portrayed the triumph of machinery over humanity and the devastation that would follow from industrialized warfare (Document 4). Such imaginings foreshadowed what war would come to be.[12]

Alongside this multifaceted fascination with war, initiatives to curtail international conflict also grew in the twenty-five years leading up to World War I. The Austrian writer Bertha von Suttner's 1889 novel *Lay Down Your Arms*, which describes the sufferings inflicted by war, became an international bestseller (Document 3). In 1905, after helping to launch a movement for disarmament, Suttner won the Nobel Peace Prize. On account of these impulses toward internationalism and pacifism, some Europeans thought war would no longer serve to resolve disputes between civilized powers. The Hague Conventions of 1899 and 1907 offered an opportunity to curtail the conduct and destructiveness of future wars (Document 2). The conventions resulted in international laws to regulate warfare on land and sea, as well as the treatment of prisoners of war. Although the conventions had limits, the achievement of codifying what was deemed appropriate for the waging of war said as much about the major powers' fears of what new weaponry and total war—involving all facets of the nation—might bring as it did about their optimism that war could be thus controlled.[13]

By 1914, unresolved tensions in the Balkans fueled mutual suspicion between the two main allied bodies in Europe—Austria-Hungary, Germany, and Italy on one side and Britain, France, and Russia on the other. Most states also faced actual or potential strife within their own borders. Volatile situations ranging from the disruption that might result from the further rise of socialist and other working-class movements to the episodic violence that accompanied specific events (such as France's Dreyfus affair and Russia's 1905 revolution) contributed to political instability. Vibrant socialist activity, especially in the form of strikes, and a vigorous feminist campaign for equal rights in many parts of Europe demonstrate that constituent bodies of various states had serious grievances against their governments and their societies. Such domestic problems could distract governments from paying attention to international affairs and also lead to anxiety about how to unify a nation to face a common external threat.

In the end, no single movement or event caused the First World War. Instead, it was the result of multiple contributing factors, including imperial conflict, an arms race on land and sea, the force of nationalism, and a willingness to accept government justifications for waging war. All helped to create an atmosphere that in the summer of 1914 fostered the outbreak of full-scale European war.

When Archduke Franz Ferdinand, heir to the Austro-Hungarian throne, and his wife, Sophie, arrived in the Bosnian capital of Sarajevo in June 1914, Austria-Hungary was already well aware of nationalist tensions in its empire. These tensions exploded on June 28 when Gavrilo Princip, a Bosnian Serb nationalist who was part of a movement that wanted to wrest Bosnia-Herzegovina away from Austria-Hungary and unite it with Serbia, fired the bullets that took the lives of the archduke and his wife. Given the entanglements of the alliance system, among other factors, the assassination of Franz Ferdinand triggered a series of events that soon threw much of Europe into turmoil.

Following the assassination, Austria-Hungary was determined to halt what it saw as Serbia's aggression in the Balkans. After securing nearly unconditional German support—a guarantee described as "the blank check"—it issued a forty-eight-hour ultimatum to the Serbian government. The government in Vienna expected that Serbia would reject its unreasonable demands, including the right of Austro-Hungarian officials to violate Serbia's sovereignty by conducting the investigation into the assassination on Serbian soil. Austria-Hungary anticipated using Serbia's rejection to declare war in hopes of both maintaining its hold in the Balkans and curtailing Serbia's nationalist ambitions. Serbia rebuffed the ultimatum on July 25, and both sides began to mobilize for armed conflict. On July 28, Austria-Hungary declared war on Serbia.

Russia quickly decided to mobilize its forces in support of Serbia. Germany saw this as a provocative and hostile move and in turn began to mobilize its military. German mobilization alerted Belgium, France, and Britain that war was imminent. A prewar German strategy for fighting enemies on two fronts by concentrating forces on one foe at a time, called the Schlieffen Plan, aimed first to attack France in the west by sending troops through neutral Belgium. This assumed that once German troops had triumphed over France, Germany could turn to its enemies on its eastern borders. At the end of July, German officials were trying to persuade the British government to stay out of the forthcoming war even if Belgium's neutrality was violated. In response, Britain asked both France and Germany for new guarantees to safeguard Belgium's neutral status, and Germany refused. France then began to mobilize. The alliance system held to a great extent: France backed Russia, which was offering support to Serbia, and Germany assisted Austria-Hungary.

Italy chose to stay out of the conflict at that moment, despite the Triple Alliance. It was not until German troops crossed the border into Belgium that Britain—after first demanding that Germany halt its attack on this neutral state—declared war on Germany.

By the end of the first week in August, the Europe of the armed camps had been transformed into a conflagration, pitting the Allied forces, led by Britain, France and Russia, against the Central Powers, dominated by Austria-Hungary and Germany. All of the major players in Europe—many of them imperial states invested in territory from Africa to Asia—were at war, an event greeted with both enthusiasm (Document 7) and trepidation (Document 8).[14]

LIVING THROUGH THE FIRST WORLD WAR

War arrived in the summer of 1914, as the largest armies ever assembled in Europe to that date poured across borders. By the war's end, millions of lives would be lost. During its course, the war affected people on nearly every continent and from every social group. Although suffering proved a common denominator across many lines, wartime experiences varied enormously. Age, class, ethnicity, gender, nationality, occupation, religion, and temperament—to start with some of the most obvious distinctions—could and did each have an enormous effect on the "kind" of war an individual encountered. One's view of the war might change because of rank in the military, duration and type of active-duty service, marital status, sexual orientation, political beliefs, and generational membership. To understand the war's consequences for both individuals and wartime societies, we must keep in mind the larger context for the individual voices expressed in the documents in part two.

When the mobilization orders went forth in July 1914, soldiers in Austria-Hungary, France, Germany, and Russia prepared for battle. After the declarations of war, crowds gathered in the main public thoroughfares of capital cities across Europe. In Britain, the one major state without a conscript army, men flocked to recruiting offices. Bands played, crowds of men and women sang and cheered, politicians spoke, women smiled through their tears, and young men marched off to war. But is this what the "mood" of 1914 was really like? Conventional versions of the war's outbreak often stress the enthusiasm that greeted its arrival, and a number of sources support this interpretation. Beyond the flag-waving throngs, however, a number of voices of dissent or caution also could be found.[15]

Britain provides a particularly interesting case for assessing the mood of 1914. It delayed entering the war for several days after the other major powers and made the violation of Belgium's neutrality by Germany its central justification. By making entry into the war a question of honor and morality—portraying the cause as defending a helpless nation that Britain had sworn to safeguard and showing Germany in the worst possible light—Britain persuaded large numbers of men to join the army voluntarily. Some of the recruitment messages also appealed to basic ideas about masculine honor in defense of women and children (Document 9). The highest rates of enlistment came from those in middle-class professions such as finance and commerce, about 40 percent of whom enlisted, versus about 28 percent of those in industrial occupations.[16] One reason for this discrepancy was anxiety among those in the laboring classes about what would happen to their families if the men, who were usually the households' breadwinners, left. This resulted in the government passing special legislation to create "separation allowances" that would provide a fixed income to soldiers' dependents, even to unmarried women and their children under certain circumstances.[17] Nearly every participant nation came up with some scheme to deliver financial aid to those who relied on a combatant's wages for survival; these measures helped alleviate some but not all of military families' initial economic problems.[18]

When troops from Britain, France, and Germany finally met in battle in August 1914, they learned that this was a new type of war, employing weapons of greater sophistication—and deadlier effect—than most of them had experienced before. Some panicked, but the British and French military were ruthless in administering justice. The peak of executions for desertion came in the first year of the war. More potent artillery and machine guns helped Allied forces hold the line, most decisively at the First Battle of the Marne (September 6–12, 1914), but these powerful and relatively new weapons caused profound injuries and a high death toll. Some of these effects could also be seen at the First Battle of Ypres (October 12–November 17, 1914).

Meanwhile in the east (see Map 2 on page 16), Russia's forces advanced across East Prussia by sheer weight of numbers, which caused Germany to send reinforcements under the combined leadership of Paul von Hindenburg and Erich von Ludendorff. At the Battle of Tannenberg in late August, German troops wiped out Russia's Second Army; the Germans then decided to press forward into Russia. To the south, Austro-Hungarian forces endured a crushing defeat by the Russians and remained unable to conquer Serbia, despite temporarily capturing Belgrade in December 1914.

December 1914 found most states facing a shortage of ammunition as many troops dug in along the western front. Despite the mythic "Christmas truce" of that year—a very brief and unofficial cease-fire during which some soldiers on both sides ventured into the area between the lines to meet in a spirit of limited but real camaraderie—miles of trenches and barbed wire transformed the landscape and led to hundreds of thousands of armed men confronting one another along an extremely long and often narrow frontier. The western front became synonymous with the misery of surviving amid mud, lice, fleas, rats, disease, and the sporadic, deadly violence that crossed what became known as "no-man's-land," the territory between the opposing lines of trenches. Map 1 shows these lines, which ran like parallel scars through Belgium and northern France for nearly four years. When the Ottoman Empire entered the war late in 1914, fighting expanded beyond the western and eastern fronts.

The growing realization at the end of 1914 that this would indeed be a protracted conflict led to new questions of how to finance the war. The prewar arms race made it seem as though ensuring an adequate supply of shells and other military equipment would not be a problem, but all sides underestimated how much wartime supplies mattered and how quickly they could be depleted. The states' ability to keep their wartime economies afloat related directly to their ability to wage war. Moreover, the hardships faced by civilians and the extent to which governments came to intervene in basic economic matters—the supply and demand of essential goods as well as wages—suggest how important economics were in winning or losing the war. States also encouraged their citizens to contribute directly to the war effort through the purchase of war bonds. Posters advertising bonds (Documents 10–12) were a key part of the propaganda that sought to link civilians and combatants experiencing this total war.[19]

Despite these efforts, segments of the population in all participant states and some neutral nations questioned the necessity for, and the costs of, war. To some extent, these voices came from socialist and feminist circles, even though officially most members of these groups embraced the war effort. Notable antiwar voices included well-known intellectual figures such as France's Romain Rolland and Britain's Bertrand Russell, the latter of whom lost his position at Cambridge University because of his pacifist views. In 1915, several international conferences took place in neutral countries such as Switzerland and the Netherlands to advocate an increased role for nonbelligerent states in bringing to fruition a negotiated end of the war. The first large international gathering of feminists since the outbreak of hostilities took place

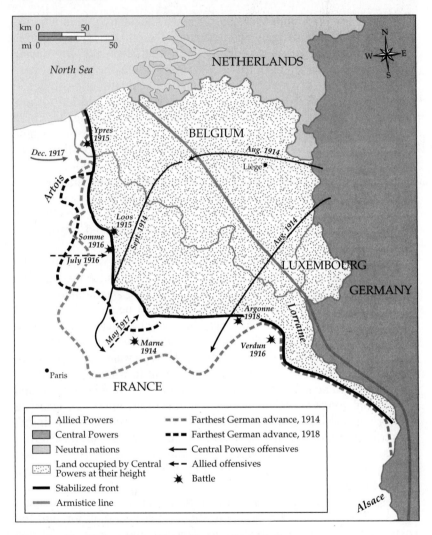

km 0   50
mi 0   50

North Sea

NETHERLANDS

N
W   E
S

Ypres
1915

BELGIUM

Dec. 1917

Aug. 1914

Liège

Artois

Loos
1915

Somme
1916

July 1916

Sept. 1914

Aug. 1914

LUXEMBOURG

GERMANY

Argonne
1918

May 1917

Marne
1914

Lorraine

Verdun
1916

Paris

FRANCE

☐ Allied Powers	– – – Farthest German advance, 1914
▨ Central Powers	▬ ▬ ▬ Farthest German advance, 1918
▨ Neutral nations	← Central Powers offensives
⬚ Land occupied by Central Powers at their height	←– Allied offensives
▬ Stabilized front	✳ Battle
▬ Armistice line	

Alsace

Map 1. *The Western Front Battle Zones, 1914–1918*

14

in The Hague beginning in April 1915 and gave rise to the Women's International League, an organization that tried to use the status of women—united in anguish and desperate to avert the harrowing grief of mothers for their fallen sons—to urge a speedy end to the war (Document 28).

Meanwhile, the scope of the war continued to expand as Italy, neglecting its earlier commitment to the Triple Alliance and having secretly been promised new territory in the war's aftermath, joined the Allied powers in May 1915. Since Italy mainly fought Austria-Hungary, the Italian war experience took place primarily in the daunting terrain of the Dolomites, or Italian Alps. Bulgaria, a state that, like Italy, had been recruited by both sides, chose to join the Central powers in the fall of 1915. This helped lead to Serbia's defeat and occupation. The United States, while officially remaining a neutral power, took advantage of France's and Britain's demands for goods, which boosted its economy. As a result, it became more closely tied to the Allies.

Even at this early stage, it was becoming evident that war on the eastern front differed substantially from that in the west. This was confirmed by the failure of the Allied offensive of 1915, one part of which was led by the British at Neuve-Chapelle in March and the other by the French near Arras in May. The Allies then decided that perhaps the best way to break the stalemate in the west would be to open up other, more active fronts. Thus came plans to take on the Ottoman Empire directly in 1915 by vigorously attacking the Gallipoli Peninsula en route to seizing Istanbul (see Map 2). Combined British and Commonwealth (largely Australian and New Zealand) forces, with some French assistance, were supposed to work in conjunction with the Royal Navy to take out defensive positions and allow an assault on Turkish territory. The Battle of Gallipoli began with naval operations in February and continued with the launching of a land invasion in April. Throughout the campaign, Allied troops also fought the climate and disease, especially dysentery. By December 1915, the last Allied forces had evacuated the peninsula, and a new Turkish hero, Mustafa Kemal (Atatürk), had emerged on the victorious side. The Allied plan had failed dismally, with a casualty rate close to 50 percent.[20]

Within the Ottoman Empire, the growing power of nationalist factions in the government contributed to a wholesale slaughter of the Armenian population, sometimes referred to as the first modern European genocide. Fearful of an uprising by the minority Armenian population (which many thought would likely be encouraged by support from Russia), the Ottoman army created a special organization to control

Map 2. *Battle Zones in Eastern and Southeastern Europe*

16

separatist impulses. The resulting massacres and forced deportations wiped out much of the state's Armenian population beginning in the spring of 1915 (Documents 24 and 25). These actions were greeted both with skepticism and outrage. The Allied powers objected to "crimes . . . against humanity and civilization," but the international community was in no position to intervene.[21]

In the war's early years, stories of the plight of prisoners of war (POWs) and those trapped behind enemy lines offered stark examples of a different type of "no-man's-land." Some Allied soldiers found themselves stuck in areas of France or Belgium that were occupied by the German army. International agreements such as the Hague Conventions, forged in the late nineteenth century, helped standardize the treatment of POWs, and a relatively benign captivity ended up being one of the more common wartime experiences. An estimated 8.5 million combatants were captured during the war, nearly three-fourths of them serving on the eastern front. Thus spending time in a POW camp was a fairly typical experience for Austro-Hungarian and Russian troops. Compared to the conditions endured by their compatriots, the hunger, labor, disease, overcrowding, and malaise experienced by POWs seemed less startling and worthy of concern.[22] In fact, the odds of survival were better in the POW camps, especially for officers, than among troops facing the most catastrophic battles of the war in the west, but the experience of captivity was still seen as humiliating and difficult (Document 19).

In occupied Belgium and northern France, inhabitants in some locales risked their lives and livelihoods to protect and assist Allied troops left behind. If caught, they could be executed as spies. There is some evidence to suggest that this was indeed what some of them were. They were not, however, the only ones engaged in espionage. On a larger scale than ever before, participant nations operated formal groups to orchestrate and coordinate espionage. An elaborate network of informants, often with little training or protection, was coaxed into being by Allied authorities in occupied Belgium and France. The British-sponsored organization called La Dame Blanche (the White Lady) recruited dozens of Belgians, including women, to record and transmit information on troop movements. Celebrated figures such as the British nurse Edith Cavell, working in Brussels, were executed for aiding Allied soldiers to escape occupied territories and return to active duty. The most famous spy of the First World War was a failed one—the "spy-seductress" Mata Hari, who was merely the most conspicuous example of what had long been regarded as a not-quite-legitimate means of waging war.[23]

Civilian refugees fleeing from advancing troops also suffered the traumas of this large-scale war. The plight of those trying to avoid or escape the invading German army in Belgium and northern France provoked a widespread humanitarian response as they fled south and, eventually for some, across the English Channel. Similarly, in the fall of 1914, thousands of refugees from Galicia arrived in Vienna, and in 1915 others would follow from regions near the Italian front. Official statistics from Russia indicate that there were more than three million refugees in that nation by the end of 1915, and by the end of the war, 5 percent of the Russian population consisted of displaced persons. While there was sympathy for their predicament, refugees could also provoke fear that they would deprive the local population of needed resources.[24]

In France, refugees from the north carried with them stories of German brutality, the mutilation of civilians, and the rape of women. The French and British governments created committees to investigate alleged German atrocities. When the official report of the Bryce Committee on Alleged German Outrages appeared in Britain in the spring of 1915, not only did it become a best-selling government document, but it also concluded in no uncertain terms that "murder, lust and pillage prevailed over many parts of Belgium on a scale unparalleled in any war between civilized nations during the last three centuries."[25] The official French investigation reached a similar conclusion.

The plight of refugees, particularly those from Belgium, became a major feature of Allied propaganda. Although abuses did occur, propaganda about conditions in Belgium and northern France often exaggerated the nature and severity of the treatment of civilians. Official propaganda, for the first time orchestrated by the government's own agencies, such as Britain's Ministry of Information, waged a war of words and images and made extensive use of Germany's alleged crimes in rallying the nation to sustain the war effort. In such propaganda, the Germans became "Huns," and the war was frequently portrayed as one pitting Western "civilisation" against a barbaric German "*Kultur*" (using the German word to suggest that this was a distortion of authentic European "culture").

This impression of German barbarism was further enhanced when, in April 1915, Germany unleashed lethal chemical warfare by using poisonous gas–filled shells at the Second Battle of Ypres. It did not take long for Britain and France to follow suit. The development and issuing of gas masks to soldiers and the deployment of chemical shells then proceeded on both sides (Documents 10 and 15). The use of chemical weapons provoked condemnation, as did wartime innovations involving submarines and aircraft.

Control of the seas was a crucial part of the Allied strategy, which included enforcing a blockade that would make Germany feel the war at home. Anglo-German rivalry over naval supremacy, or at least Britain's perception that Germany threatened its long-standing dominance of the oceans, was a key factor in creating hostility between the two states before the war. The sinking of Allied vessels and other ships, especially the passenger ship *Lusitania* in May 1915, by German U-boats, or submarines, became acts of infamy on the Allied side. However, the most decisive naval battle of the war took place in 1916, when the German and British fleets clashed in the Battle of Jutland. Despite the fact that Germany inflicted more damage on the British in terms of destruction of ships and loss of life, at the end of the battle Britain maintained control of the high seas and was thus able to continue the blockade. The questions then became how effective submarine warfare could become and whether Germany was willing to risk alienating international public opinion and antagonizing the United States by resuming it in an unrestricted form.[26] Not until January 1917 did Germany, after much debate, resume its unrestricted U-boat attacks, a decision that contributed to the United States' willingness to enter the war several months later.

World War I was also the first war to make extensive use of innovations in aeronautics. At first, aircraft mainly helped with surveillance; at the start of the war airplanes were deemed of little use in conducting aerial attacks. This was not the case with the large airships known as zeppelins. Germany began using zeppelins to conduct aerial attacks at the outset of the war. By 1915, airplanes were being used in both air raids and plane-to-plane combat, and by 1917 military uses of aircraft had become a crucial feature of the war.[27] The loudest condemnation of military aviation came with the attacks on civilian populations. Although the number of non-combatants killed in air raids paled in comparison with the death toll on more traditional battlefields, the fact that these casualties included women and children far removed from active battle zones produced anguished responses. The assessment of these attacks as atrocities against helpless innocents by depraved barbarians could hardly be maintained when states under attack retaliated with reprisals. Before long, a new kind of hero—the fighter pilot, or "ace"—had emerged, and with the mounting number of civilian deaths, aerial attacks became another item with which to condemn one's enemies and rally support for the war. As they withstood aerial onslaughts, civilians of all ages and sexes now had the opportunity to act heroically and to show the importance of steadfast morale at home (Document 33).[28]

Wartime governments further adapted to modern warfare by intervening ever more deeply in their societies' economies. A variety of industries came directly under state control in the United Kingdom, the final death knell for laissez-faire economics, and various governments, including those in France and Germany, also determined which skilled workers would be exempt from military service in order to keep munitions factories operational. In Britain and France, the nation's leadership changed hands without an election and resulted in the elevation of politicians deemed more likely to pursue the war to a successful end. In Britain, David Lloyd George took over as prime minister from Herbert Asquith in December 1916, while Georges Clemenceau replaced Paul Painlevé as premier of France in November 1917. These states and others also greatly curtailed civil liberties and freedom of the press as well as the free-market economy.

Efforts to manage the food supply further demonstrated widespread government intervention in the economy. Germany became one of the first nations to resort to rationing. In January 1915, the German government began to ration bread; soon other basic foodstuffs, such as milk, meat, butter, and other fats, joined the list. By 1916, the state imposed a system of general rationing throughout Germany. When the supply of potatoes—the main substitute for wheat—diminished, Germans had to turn to turnips during the winter of 1916–1917, which became known as "the turnip winter." As the caloric intake of German civilians fell, this had political as well as health consequences. Hungry people frustrated by the long hours of waiting in line for food that did not always materialize became increasingly vocal in their criticism of the government and the war (Document 27).[29] Poor harvests in Austria-Hungary also contributed to the development of rationing there, where bread became subject to quotas as early as April 1915. Like Germany, Austria-Hungary soon limited access to coffee, milk, fats, and sugar. Other states resisted outright rationing. France imposed price controls in 1916 but only began to ration sugar, bread, and flour in the summer of 1918. Italy resisted rationing until 1917, and in Britain efforts to expand food production delayed the imposition of rationing. By early 1918, however, the British government was regulating access to sugar, meat, and fats.

Supplies intended for troops were already being rationed, and civilians were continually urged to send packages to the front containing tobacco, warm knitted socks, and other items that would give material comfort to soldiers, along with morale-sustaining letters. Charitable organizations sprang up to supply these and other items to soldiers on a regular basis. The official rations of food, alcohol, and tobacco allowed to members of the military reveal a good deal about varying expectations of their needs. Lists of official rations for British, Indian, and German troops show both the regimented nature of military life and the enormous amount of organization required to keep soldiers supplied with basic necessities. They also indicate how much the war experience differed between colonial and regular troops. For example, Indian troops received less meat but more spices. For most European troops, alcohol and tobacco were a standard part of the daily rations. In 1914, for example, daily rations for German troops included "two cigars and two cigarettes or 1 oz. pipe tobacco, or 9/10 oz. plug tobacco, or 1/5 oz. snuff; and, at discretion of commanding officer: 0.17 pint spirits, 0.44 pint wine, 0.88 pint beer." German troops also received meat, sugar, and coffee—although after June 1916, even members of the military had meatless days. In 1914, British troops could expect meat, sugar, and tea (rather than coffee) daily, as well as a ration of spirits or porter equivalent to 1/2 gill of rum (also at the commanding officer's discretion) and a daily allotment "not exceeding 2 oz. tobacco per week." Neither tobacco nor alcohol was made available to Indian troops in the British army, and they were allotted much less meat and tea, although their daily rations did include "4 oz. dhall; 2 oz. ghee; 1/6 oz. chillies; 1/6 oz. turmeric; 1/3 oz. ginger; 1/6 oz. garlic"—all items not available to other British troops.[30]

The duration of the war led to other dramatic changes in policy. In 1916, Britain succumbed to its military manpower shortage by introducing conscription, although with the exclusion of Ireland so as not to provoke nationalists there. With its arrival came another innovation of the war: the conscientious objector. Legislation authorizing conscription allowed a provision to be made for those who were pacifists on account of conscience or religion. This was not, however, an easy thing to define. To prevent "shirking," the government formed tribunals to evaluate the claims of those seeking the status of conscientious objector. Some were willing to serve in noncombatant, and particularly in medical, roles. Yet some of those who agreed to nonmilitary service nonetheless found themselves sent into battle. Not all who sought conscientious-objector status were granted it. Some were turned down and ordered into the armed forces; if they refused to go, they were sent to prison and often treated very harshly there. A new expression, *conchie*, became a pejorative name for those who opted for this alternative.[31]

Concern with maintaining both military and civilian morale led to the widespread suppression of dissenting voices and the curtailing of free speech and a free press even in liberal regimes such as those in France and Britain. One clear example of this can be found in Britain's Defence of the Realm Act (1914), which gave the state the power to imprison people for spreading information likely to harm His Majesty's forces or the war effort and to restrict the movement of the population. The Defence of the Realm Act even brought back the basic provisions of the controversial nineteenth-century Contagious Diseases Act, once again making it a criminal offense for any woman to "infect a member of His Majesty's Forces or the Forces of His Majesty's Allies with a venereal disease."[32]

The term *home front* was another invention of the First World War. While it suggests the ample opportunities for contributing to the war effort available to civilians, especially women, it also implies the separation of these experiences from those on some more "authentic" *front line*. In many wartime states, women's labor was essential to the war effort. It could involve extensive activities in traditional roles, such as nursing (Document 20), as well as in more unconventional ones, such as police work and even, in Russia, combat. Women's replacement of mobilized men in wartime factories performing grueling and dangerous work was lauded by their governments but defined as being only "for the duration." For many women, working for wages was nothing new; what had shifted was the nature of their work. Public attention often focused on women who had no financial incentive to work but did so out of patriotism and duty (Document 30). In spite of the encouragement for women to work outside the home, widespread wartime concern with women's morality, sexuality, and maternity demonstrates the extent to which perceptions about the changing role of women provoked anxiety in states mobilized for total war.[33]

In addition to calling on women to play a vital role in sustaining the war effort, belligerent states also turned to their colonial subjects. While the war may have started in Europe, it quickly spread to European colonies (see Map 3). More than two million Africans participated in the war, some as soldiers and others in the labor force; more than 200,000 died in action.[34] The French conscripted soldiers from West Africa and used them, to some extent, as shock troops on the western front. France also relied on Indochina to supply wartime labor. The British made use of what it deemed the "martial races" of India and of military personnel and laborers from the West Indies (Documents 17 and 18). Colonial troops of European descent—Zoaves from Algeria, for example, as well

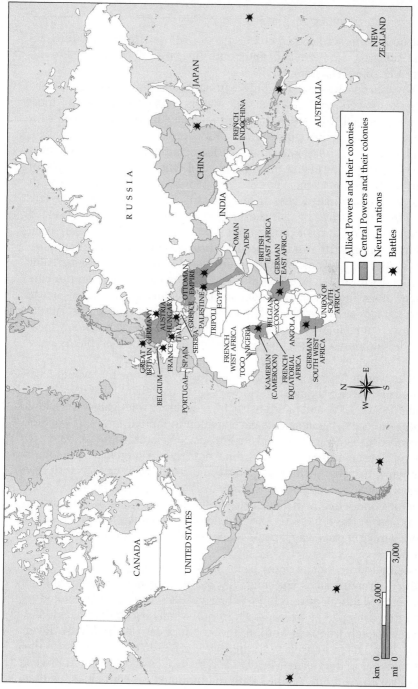

Map 3. *Global Battle Zones, 1914–1918*

Allied Powers and their colonies

Central Powers and their colonies

Neutral nations

Battles

NEW ZEALAND

AUSTRALIA

JAPAN

FRENCH INDOCHINA

CHINA

RUSSIA

INDIA

OMAN

ADEN

BRITISH EAST AFRICA

GERMAN EAST AFRICA

OTTOMAN EMPIRE

PALESTINE

EGYPT

TRIPOLI

GREECE

SERBIA

AUSTRIA-HUNGARY

GERMANY

GREAT BRITAIN

ITALY

FRANCE

SPAIN

PORTUGAL

BELGIUM

FRENCH WEST AFRICA

TOGO

NIGERIA

KAMERUN (CAMEROON)

FRENCH EQUATORIAL AFRICA

BELGIAN CONGO

ANGOLA

GERMAN SOUTH WEST AFRICA

UNION OF SOUTH AFRICA

N E S W

CANADA

UNITED STATES

km 0   3,000

mi 0   3,000

as troops from across the settler societies of the British Empire (Canada, Australia, New Zealand, and South Africa)—all contributed to the war in Europe (Document 50).

Yet, Europe was not the only battleground. European states were imperial powers, and this war was fought in the far reaches of their empires as well.[35] In Africa, the war took place both by proxy and with the assistance of European powers. Its people and resources contributed to the war effort both on the African continent, which was almost entirely under European imperial control, and on the battlefields of Europe. Since the Central powers' naval forces could not compete with the Allies', German access to its African colonies was severely limited. In West Africa, British and French colonial troops quickly seized control of the German protectorate Togoland in 1914 and Cameroon (Kamerun) in 1916. War in East Africa proved a different and more difficult matter for all sides. Fighting there lasted until late 1918, at a greater cost and with more extensive destruction than elsewhere on the continent. Even though Allied troops included soldiers from India; South, East, and West Africa; the Belgian Congo; and Portuguese East Africa, they were unable to gain control of German East Africa in a timely manner. In addition, climate, disease, and communication problems hampered all military engagements in sub-Saharan Africa.[36]

The war in Asia was very much a sideshow, but one that would have consequences for the next world war. Japan had allied itself with Great Britain since 1902, and in August 1914, it declared war against Germany. From the start, Japan saw its participation in limited terms. It was not prepared to send military aid to Europe, but it used the occasion to attack German fortifications in China, notably in Tsingtao. Unlike other participants, Japan achieved a short and impressive victory with few losses and welcomed its troops home by the end of 1914. Japan's victory gave it confidence as it began to pursue opportunities to consolidate its power in the region. By the middle of the conflict, few other states were similarly placed as Japan's economy also grew enormously during the war.[37]

As the governments of the participant nations began to adjust to the altered circumstances and longevity of this war, military leaders kept looking for a breakthrough. In February 1916, Germany attempted to end the stalemate on the western front. Its military leaders decided to target French troops at Verdun, the key fortress on the Meuse River (see Map 1). On February 21, the Battle of Verdun began. Despite the calculations of the German leaders and in the face of tremendous losses, the French held out. As the death toll mounted on both sides, neither

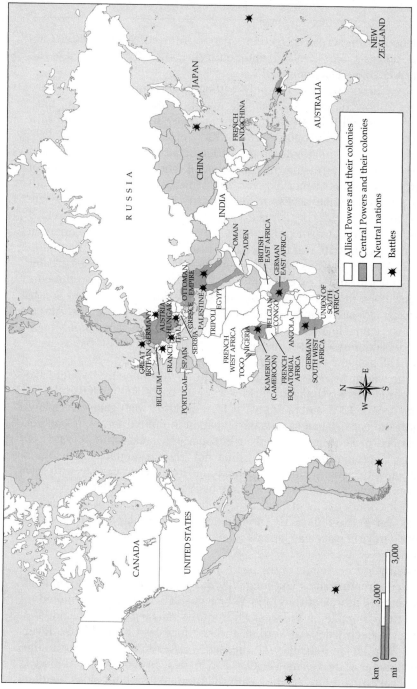

Map 3. *Global Battle Zones, 1914–1918*

as troops from across the settler societies of the British Empire (Canada, Australia, New Zealand, and South Africa) — all contributed to the war in Europe (Document 50).

Yet, Europe was not the only battleground. European states were imperial powers, and this war was fought in the far reaches of their empires as well.[35] In Africa, the war took place both by proxy and with the assistance of European powers. Its people and resources contributed to the war effort both on the African continent, which was almost entirely under European imperial control, and on the battlefields of Europe. Since the Central powers' naval forces could not compete with the Allies', German access to its African colonies was severely limited. In West Africa, British and French colonial troops quickly seized control of the German protectorate Togoland in 1914 and Cameroon (Kamerun) in 1916. War in East Africa proved a different and more difficult matter for all sides. Fighting there lasted until late 1918, at a greater cost and with more extensive destruction than elsewhere on the continent. Even though Allied troops included soldiers from India; South, East, and West Africa; the Belgian Congo; and Portuguese East Africa, they were unable to gain control of German East Africa in a timely manner. In addition, climate, disease, and communication problems hampered all military engagements in sub-Saharan Africa.[36]

The war in Asia was very much a sideshow, but one that would have consequences for the next world war. Japan had allied itself with Great Britain since 1902, and in August 1914, it declared war against Germany. From the start, Japan saw its participation in limited terms. It was not prepared to send military aid to Europe, but it used the occasion to attack German fortifications in China, notably in Tsingtao. Unlike other participants, Japan achieved a short and impressive victory with few losses and welcomed its troops home by the end of 1914. Japan's victory gave it confidence as it began to pursue opportunities to consolidate its power in the region. By the middle of the conflict, few other states were similarly placed as Japan's economy also grew enormously during the war.[37]

As the governments of the participant nations began to adjust to the altered circumstances and longevity of this war, military leaders kept looking for a breakthrough. In February 1916, Germany attempted to end the stalemate on the western front. Its military leaders decided to target French troops at Verdun, the key fortress on the Meuse River (see Map 1). On February 21, the Battle of Verdun began. Despite the calculations of the German leaders and in the face of tremendous losses, the French held out. As the death toll mounted on both sides, neither the Germans nor the French were willing to concede defeat. By late June, French casualties reached 275,000 and those of Germany 240,000. In the end, the ability of the French to stand their ground was counted as a kind of victory. But at what cost? The longest field battle in history had also produced the largest number of casualties per square yard of battleground (Documents 21 and 23).[38]

Meantime, the British and French had been developing their own ideas for mounting an offensive at the point where their respective lines joined in the Somme. The implementation of this plan in the summer of 1916 followed the four-month-long German assault on Verdun. Thinking that the Germans could be close to exhausting their reserves, Britain and its allies added troops in the Somme and planned to shell the German trenches ceaselessly, knocking out their artillery and barbed wire. They would thereby render the occupants of the trenches unable to use their machine guns and grenades. When the call to go over the top came, Allied foot soldiers could then cross no-man's-land, take the German trenches, push ahead, and break the enemy lines. It was not an implausible plan, but little attention had been paid to what would happen if the bombardment did not succeed in neutralizing the Germans.

July 1, the first day of battle on the Somme for the British, was a total disaster. Of the 60,000 men who went over the top in the first waves, half were casualties within thirty minutes. Of the 120,000 who attacked that day, the casualty rate was near 50 percent, or 57,470 troops, 19,240 of whom were killed.[39] The German positions had not collapsed, and as British attackers advanced across the divide, they faced a seemingly endless stream of rifle and machine-gun fire from behind the still-fortified trenches. The horror of the situation was made worse by the fact that the wounded were so numerous as to overwhelm the casualty clearing stations and other medical facilities. Many men had to be left bleeding in the middle of no-man's-land until dark, when it was safer to go and collect them. In the longest case on record, one wounded survivor waited between the trenches for fourteen days; many others died because they were not treated quickly enough.[40]

When the realization of the immense failure of July 1 hit the British high command, its reaction was to begin to regroup and start afresh, to continue to try an offensive push. The result was a battle that lasted from July until nearly the end of 1916. The British launched ninety mainly small-scale attacks between mid-July and mid-September; they resulted in gains of less than three square miles of ground at the cost of 82,000 casualties.[41] On September 15, they introduced a new weapon—the tank—in hopes of achieving a breakthrough. In its initial deployment, the tank proved mechanically unreliable. Furthermore, the rain that fell consistently across northern France that autumn helped turn the entire battlefield into a mud bath. By the time the offensive was finally halted, it was regarded as a failure. Britain had suffered 420,000 casualties, France 200,000, and Germany around 500,000.

As if the losses on the Somme were not enough, Britain faced internal upheaval in 1916 as well. In April, a group of Irish nationalists striving to create an independent Ireland launched the short-lived Easter Rising, which represented a significant if ultimately fruitless challenge to British authority. Nonetheless, it reminded Britain of the danger of internal threats to the war effort, especially because some of the Irish nationalists had sought aid from Germany. The subsequent execution of the rebellion's male leaders became a rallying cry for Irish nationalist organizations such as Sinn Féin (Ourselves Alone).[42]

On the eastern front, 1916 witnessed the Brusilov offensives, pitting Russian troops against Austro-Hungarian forces in the Carpathians (see Map 2). The first phase led to spectacular success for the Russians; the Austrian Fourth Army went from having 110,000 men to 18,000 in a matter of days, due to a combination of casualties and men being taken prisoner. In response, the Central powers regrouped under largely German command and repulsed subsequent efforts by the Russians to advance, but by the close of 1916, Austria-Hungary's troops were no longer an offensive force. The final cost: 1.5 million Austro-Hungarians either killed, wounded, or captured, with Russia itself sacrificing close to a million men.[43] Victory here, as in the west, was not in sight.

In the aftermath of these military errors and failures, early 1917 was truly a winter of discontent. War weariness seemed endemic. Bread riots and economic protests increased in Germany and Russia. Mutinies took place among Italian, Russian, Austrian, and French forces. The most widespread mutinies among the French came in the spring of 1917, with incidents in 68 of the army's 112 divisions, coinciding with civilian strikes by munitions workers and others.[44] Such events did not necessarily reflect opposition to the war in general or a willingness to agree to a negotiated settlement. Instead, they seemed to indicate a deepening frustration with specific military conduct and with the length of the war.

A classic British cartoon voices an opinion that would have been deemed unthinkable (and unprintable) before the end of 1917. It depicts an encounter between two enlisted men in the trenches. The first asks, "'ow long you up for Bill?" "Seven years" is the answer, to which his friend replies, "You're lucky—I'm duration." This reflects the feeling of many combatants that the war would go on forever. Yet any talk of a negotiated peace could be deemed unpatriotic, even treasonous. In

France, the autumn of 1917 witnessed the arrival of a new crime, "defeatism," or the advocating of anything except fighting on until victory. In Germany, the government arrested socialists such as Clara Zetkin and Rosa Luxemburg for trying to organize working-class women against the war.

Nor did the death tolls diminish in 1917. The Third Battle of Ypres (commonly known as the Battle of Passchendaele) lasted from July 31 to November 10. The entire enterprise was affected by miserable weather, and by the battle's end Britain had suffered 275,000 casualties, including 70,000 deaths, for no discernible gain.[45] The brutal alpine campaign in Italy also saw renewed action (Document 22). At the Battle of Caporetto in the fall of 1917, Italy faced a near collapse as a combined Austro-Hungarian and German offensive pushed Italian troops back to just twenty miles from Venice, at a cost to the Italian army of 40,000 dead, 280,000 taken prisoner, and 350,000 deserters. Such a catastrophe actually helped avert potential revolutionary action in Italy by turning the war into a defensive contest to restore Italian territory and honor.[46]

Desperate conditions caused the Russian war effort to collapse in 1917 and also brought the return of revolution to that nation. The Russian Revolution began early in the year with strikes by women workers in Petrograd (St. Petersburg), which quickly escalated into a general strike as food riots and demonstrations against the war spread. As word of these actions reached those in the military, many troops mutinied. Unable to secure support, the Romanov dynasty toppled quickly, ending the rule of the tsars. Out of the remnants of the Duma (Russia's legislative body created in 1905) arose the Provisional Government. Then, in April, the Germans sent exiled Russian revolutionary and Bolshevik leader Vladimir Ilyich Lenin on a sealed train to Petrograd, helping transform the revolution into a contest between the Provisional Government, still committed to keeping Russia in an increasingly unpopular war, and the Bolsheviks, led by Lenin, who promised "Peace, Land and Bread." We can see Lenin's vision for Russia's future and strategy for gaining power in his April Theses (Document 35). Recognized as the legitimate government of Russia by its allies Britain, France, and the United States—the last of which declared war on Germany on April 6—the Provisional Government, under the leadership of Aleksandr Kerensky after May 1917, tried to continue the war effort in the face of enormous internal opposition. It even allowed women to serve as combat forces during the summer of 1917.

After months of unrest, the Bolsheviks wrested power from the Provisional Government in October. By December, they had signed an armistice with Germany. This did not end the fighting, as negotiations stalled and German troops continued to advance. It took until March 1918 for the Treaty of Brest-Litovsk to be concluded. Under its terms, Lenin ceded enormous swaths of territory to Germany, including Finland; parts of Poland; the Baltic states of Estonia, Lithuania, and Latvia; and territory in the Ukraine.

After the Russian Revolution, and certainly after Russia pulled out of the war, the international political dynamic changed. The United States, whose president Woodrow Wilson had campaigned in 1916 on having kept the country out of the war, had now joined Britain and France in a conflict that Wilson tried to redefine as one to make the world "safe for democracy." Although America could not instantly train, equip, and deploy its troops, it could make an even more vital economic contribution to the Allied war effort.[47]

In the meantime, Germany now faced a one-front war and could turn its full attention to breaking the impasse in the west. Thus Germany's spring offensive of 1918 came as no surprise. In light of growing dissent at home, Germany's leaders also felt that the war had to be won quickly. By early 1918, strikes affected much of the nation, and some were even calling for the end of the kaiser and his government. This opposition grew more pronounced as a result of the food shortages and growing hunger in German cities and the mounting death tolls on the battlefield (Document 32). The German army came close to achieving a crushing blow in the spring push that finally broke the stalemate on the western front, but it stalled when it overran its supply lines. At home, the Central powers continued to fall apart. War weariness, as well as the lack of food, fuel, and hope, contributed to the collapse of their war efforts at home.[48]

The war waged in 1918 was once again a war of movement and, for the soldiers active in its skirmishes, deadlier than many long months of trench warfare. New long-range German artillery fired on the city of Paris, and this, in addition to air raids, made life there more dangerous, causing inhabitants to flee and resulting in the loss of life and property. Significantly, however, it did not sufficiently weaken morale or cause civilians there to revolt. The arrival of American troops—nearly 1.5 million in the last six months of the war—also had a profound psychological effect. These self-confident, if untested, soldiers provided welcome relief for the French and British troops who had long been in the field.

By the time the guns fell silent on the eleventh hour of the eleventh day of the eleventh month in 1918, the Central Powers faced a political crisis. The Austro-Hungarian Empire was splintering; Czechoslovakia had declared itself an independent state, and Croatia and Hungary soon followed. A series of revolts—among sailors at the German naval base in Kiel, among workers and starving civilians in major cities such as Berlin—prompted the worker-led German Socialist party to declare a republic as Kaiser Wilhelm II fled the country on November 9. Similarly, Russia was now facing a bloody civil war that would last until 1921. The brutal fighting between the Bolsheviks and their opponents accelerated the pace at which all aspects of the Russian state came under the control of the Communist party, displaced millions of civilians, destroyed communities and lives, and set this nation (and the world) on a very different path. As was the case when war had been declared, cheering crowds filled the streets of the cities of the major participant states on November 11, 1918. But overwhelming relief and joy at the war's end could neither mask the losses nor obscure the costs.

THE WAR'S END AND AFTERMATH

As is the case with its origins, the First World War's end and consequences continue to inspire debate. Given the enormous death tolls and material damage, the postwar world faced several key questions. How were the war's losses to be borne? How could participants be compensated? How could the circumstances that had led to the war be avoided in the future?

Before a formal peace settlement could be concluded, the long process of demobilization began. In contrast to the relative rapidity with which troops were mobilized for the war, the process by which troops came home was quite slow, even more so for prisoners of war than for regular troops. Some soldiers remained at their posts in areas not firmly under the control of the victors in November 1918, such as British troops stationed in the Middle East and French troops sent into Alsace and Lorraine, territories conquered by Germany in 1870 that France now welcomed back. After June 1919, other French troops, which included colonial forces, occupied sectors of Germany. The presence of nonwhite troops among the occupiers provoked racist fears. In an international campaign to condemn France for these actions, the situation was described as the "black horror on the Rhine" (Document 44). In Germany, some returning soldiers did not disarm and rejoin civilian life at once, but instead became Freikorps, a "freelance" military threat to revolutionaries and no friend to the newly established Weimar Republic.

Fighting continued elsewhere in the east, not only in Germany and Russia but also in the states carved out of the former empires, such as

Poland and Czechoslovakia. Hungary experienced a short-lived communist revolution in 1919 that was put down in part by an invading Roma-
nian army. The prospect of revolution continued to loom over Europe.[49]

The war's formal diplomatic settlement began when the leaders of
the four victorious powers—Georges Clemenceau of France, David
Lloyd George of Britain, Vittorio Orlando of Italy, and Woodrow Wilson of the United States—came together in January 1919 at the Paris
Peace Conference to orchestrate the terms that might resolve the conflict at long last. Each nation had an agenda. Italy, for example, hoped
that its shift from the Triple Alliance to the Allies when entering the
war in 1915 would be amply rewarded, and France wanted compensa-
tion for the damages it had sustained. Wilson's widely circulated Fourteen Points offered one model for how the war might produce a lasting
and, in his words, "non-punitive" peace. His vision included the idea of
an international body, the League of Nations, to mediate and prevent
future conflicts, and the desire to create a postwar world where "self-
determination" for peoples resolved the grievances that had plagued
minorities in multinational states. These ideas evoked homegrown criticism from those concerned about America's increasing involvement in
overseas affairs (Document 42).

By this time, Lloyd George had been reelected as prime minister in
December 1918 by vowing to keep Britain's domestic wartime coalition together. Clemenceau had called for and received an overwhelming vote of confidence in the French legislature, in order to strengthen
his position at the conference. He was determined to preserve the wartime alliance against Germany, since he still saw the French republic
to which he was devoted as having the most to fear from the neighbor
who had invaded it twice (in 1870 and 1914). Orlando knew that popular opinion in Italy demanded that his state be given territory, such as
the Adriatic port of Fiume, that it had been promised secretly when it
had agreed to join Britain and France. Wilson opposed this, and in the
end Italian nationalists remained dissatisfied with the limited territorial
gains granted the country. Wilson optimistically assumed that his time
at the conference would be relatively short. Yet he ended up staying
in Paris for much of the period between January and June 1919, and
he soon became frustrated by what he saw as the intransigence of his
allies, especially France.[50]

After six months of negotiations, the major powers signed the Treaty
of Versailles (Document 43), the major peace settlement with Germany,
in the Palace of Versailles's famous Hall of Mirrors on June 28, 1919. This
document would decisively define and shape the postwar era. As Wilson

had demanded, it established the League of Nations, a body of member states dedicated to the prevention of war through such means as promoting disarmament, resolving difficult territorial disputes, and supervising postwar imperialism so as to avoid conflict between colonizing states. This treaty, as well as subsequent ones with Austria-Hungary and the Ottoman Empire, helped redraw the map of Europe, leaving some disputed territory, such as the city of Danzig (Gdansk), in the hands of the League itself. It did nothing to diminish the imperial holdings of the victors; indeed, Britain and France gained control of some of Germany's former colonies as the latter was stripped of its imperial possessions. So while the League of Nations promoted the "self-determination" of many Europeans, it did not extend this right to colonial subjects. Committed to seeing the League established, Wilson was willing to accept terms of the treaty that belied the idea of a "non-punitive" peace. Thus the final treaty deliberately penalized Germany.[51]

Article 231 of the treaty proclaimed that the war and all damages resulting from it were Germany's fault. As a result, Germany had to make amends, most notably in the form of financial reparations. Separate provisions of the treaty called for the virtual destruction of Germany's military power on land, sea, and air, as well as the elimination of military training and conscription. Some regions of Germany, such as the Rhineland, were demilitarized, and others were subject to occupation by the "Allied and Associated Governments," most notably the French. The Germans viewed the treaty as humiliating, and those worried about its long-term consequences called it the "peace to end all peace."

Thanks to this and other subsequent treaties, much of the territory in central Europe gained a new status, that of independent states no longer part of larger empires. From Estonia, Latvia, and Lithuania in the Baltic to a reconfigured Poland, from the greatly reduced and now autonomous nations of Austria and Hungary, to new states such as Czechoslovakia and Yugoslavia, the map of Europe had been redrawn. When final arrangements about the sovereignty of disputed territories emerged in the early 1920s, losing states such as Bulgaria found their claims ignored, while Romania and Greece both gained significant territory, as did Serbia, the core of the new state of Yugoslavia.[52] One consequence of the war was a wave of migration, as "minority" populations in some states were transferred to others. Thus, for example, 1.3 million Greeks "returned" to Greece, and some 400,000 Turks and 200,000 Bulgarians joined Turkey.[53]

A series of agreements concluded during and after the war also reshaped what became known as the Middle East. The Ottoman Empire had lost control of its possessions in that region and would soon emerge as modern Turkey under the leadership of Mustafa Kemal (Atatürk) in 1923. Foreseeing this empire's demise, the British and French had secretly concluded the Sykes-Picot Agreement in 1916, dividing Ottoman territories in the east between themselves (Document 45). A year later, the Balfour Declaration committed Britain, with the support of the United States and France, to sanction the Zionist aim of a Jewish homeland in Palestine (Document 46). Both documents had an important effect on the postwar settlement.[54] A formal peace agreement with the Ottoman Empire took some time to achieve, with the 1920 Treaty of Sèvres eventually being replaced by the 1923 Treaty of Lausanne. The final settlement gave new control over long-disputed territory in North Africa to Britain and France, now acting under the auspices of the League of Nations. As was the case in Europe, a series of new states emerged in the Middle East, including Iraq, Lebanon, Transjordan, Palestine, and Syria. Many of the non-Turkish populations of the Ottoman Empire now found themselves, often unhappily, within the imperial orbit of either Britain (Palestine, Iraq, and Transjordan) or France (Syria and Lebanon).[55]

Other territories came under the control of the new international body. While the League of Nations was crippled from the outset by the U.S. Senate's failure to ratify the Treaty of Versailles, which ensured that the most powerful postwar state was never a member, the League did manage to exercise some authority. For instance, it made many new non-European states "mandates" instead of colonies. Under the mandate system, either the League itself or a state given that power would administer a given territory until such time as its population was deemed capable of self-rule. In the end, the postwar settlement produced different categories of mandates, including the territories in the Middle East described in the previous paragraph. In Africa, Germany's former colonies were dispersed among Belgium, France, Britain, and South Africa. In the Pacific, various mandates were given to Japan, Australia, and New Zealand.[56]

Given this redistribution of empires and power, the economic consequences of the peace varied. All participant nations faced the costs of the war: lives lost or shattered, material damage, the destruction of property and key industries. Of active participants, the United States was in the best financial shape. The defeated powers all faced extremely difficult situations, but even victors such as France and Britain confronted the challenges of postwar reconstruction and substantial debt. The decision to force Germany to pay reparations meant that France and, to a lesser extent, Britain would receive money to help compensate them for wartime losses and to finance rebuilding efforts. In the end, Germany, its economy in shambles, never paid even close to the full amount of the reparations that had been demanded. Nonetheless, it took the Dawes Plan of 1924 and the influx of U.S. money to help the German economy even start to recover. Over time, however, most of the participant states regained some of their prewar prosperity.

This was a total war not only in economic terms but also in terms of establishing and eroding the divide between war and home fronts, combatants and civilians, and men and women. British women over age thirty, who were able to vote for the first time in December 1918, were not the only women to acquire broader political rights at the war's end. Women gained the franchise in most postwar states, with the notable exception of France.[57] Many politicians justified this act as a reward for women's wartime service and sacrifices, thus avoiding giving credit to feminists or the vibrant international movement for women's suffrage before the war.[58] In Europe, only Finnish and Norwegian women had possessed the vote prior to World War I, although women in Australia and New Zealand, still imperial subjects of Britain, also had this right. The first major wartime state to grant women's suffrage on terms equal to male suffrage was Russia's Provisional Government in the summer of 1917, although this quickly became a moot point for the entire population. The Weimar Republic gave voting rights to German women, as did many of the new states created from the former Austro-Hungarian Empire, including Austria, Czechoslovakia, Hungary, and Poland. What women did with their newfound eligibility is harder to gauge. Some postwar legislation, in states such as Italy and Britain, expanded women's access to the professions, but this did not fundamentally transform the female labor market or larger views about the value of women's waged work (Document 47).[59]

The war's cultural legacy was similarly complicated. Modernism came into greater prominence in elite postwar art and literature, as did offshoots of this prewar movement such as surrealism. From the fragmented images of the landscape of this war came artistic movements that rejected overt meaning and logic (Document 49). Works dealing with the war years themselves were briefly in vogue, then died away, only to reemerge at the end of the twenties following publication of Erich Maria Remarque's wildly successful novel *Im Westen nichts Neues* (*All Quiet on the Western Front*) in 1928 (Document 51). By 1929, Remarque's novel detailing the wartime experiences of a young German soldier and his comrades had been translated into English and other European languages; Ernest Hemingway's best-selling novel *A Farewell to Arms* had appeared; and popular autobiographical accounts of the war, such as the British writer Robert Graves's *Good-bye to All That*, were on bookshelves. Within a year, novelist Evadne Price, writing under the pseudonym Helen Zenna Smith, published a feminist response to Remarque, *Not So Quiet . . .* (Document 52). Both *All Quiet on the Western Front* and *Not So Quiet . . .* have as much to say about the generation that came of age during and after the war as about the war itself, but neither shies away from depicting the war's horror and corruption of innocence. By the mid-thirties, memoirs of the war by women such as Vera Brittain, in her widely acclaimed *Testament of Youth* (1933), showed the war in realist terms quite unlike the more oblique reflections of wartime violence and its consequences in poetry by T. S. Eliot and novels by Virginia Woolf, among others.[60]

The cultural memory of the war was shaped not only by elite paintings and literature but perhaps even more so by the widespread appearance of commemorative art in the form of war memorials and the ceremonies that accompanied them. Some lucky few emerged from the war relatively unscathed, but European nations, and to a lesser extent the rest of the states that had participated, were filled with grieving families and communities.[61] All across the participant states, the question of how to cope with the immense losses arose as soon as the first wartime deaths occurred and had intensified by war's end. In each belligerent state and former state, the public took on the task of how its dead should be commemorated and what role different constituencies (religious, military, public, private, familial) should play in these arrangements. Perhaps most dramatically, several states buried an "unknown" soldier or warrior, whose unidentified body could stand in for the many missing of the war. Such memorials were erected in London, Paris, Rome, and Washington, D.C. Britain also created a cenotaph, or empty tomb, symbolically placed along Whitehall in London to serve as a focal point of mourning and commemoration. Large numbers of combatants' bodies were not repatriated, due to either law (some countries prohibited this) or choice, with some of the bereaved opting to leave loved ones in the company of their fallen comrades. Battlefield cemeteries came to have their own monuments, such as rolls of honor (lists of the dead), and local, regional, national, and institutional war memorials were built as tangible reminders of the war's losses in the postwar world.

The First World War shattered millions of lives. In the popular memory, these deaths and injuries are perhaps all the more heartrending because this war has become associated with futility, waste, and the sacrifice of innocence. Yet, whatever lessons might be learned from this conflict must begin with an appreciation of its experiences as well as immediate and long-term legacies. Given their diversity, these legacies remain difficult to summarize. Clearly, the war contributed to an altered cultural, demographic, economic, social, and political landscape across the European continent. Some states emerged stronger than ever before, confident in their new global status. Some nations rose out of the ashes of imperial collapse. And some faced temporary setbacks, only to recover markedly in the decades ahead. On the individual level, the war left few participants untouched. What survivors made of themselves in the postwar world depended on a wide variety of characteristics, including age, class, ethnicity, gender, geographic location, health, nationality, personality, religious faith, and, above all, the circumstances of the particular war that each had waged.

NOTES

[1]The phrase "imagined community," which has become shorthand for signaling the cultural basis of nationalism, comes from Benedict Anderson, *Imagined Communities: Reflections on the Origins and Spread of Nationalism* (London: Verso, 1983). For other valuable interpretations of nationalism, see the essays in Geoff Eley and Ronald Grigor Suny, eds., *Becoming National: A Reader* (Oxford, U.K.: Oxford University Press, 1996).

[2]Giuseppe Mazzini, *The Duties of Man and Other Essays* (London: Dent, 1961).

[3]In France, by contrast, nationality was based on where one was born. A useful comparison of the differences between German and French national identity can be found in Rogers Brubaker, *Citizenship and Nationhood in France and Germany* (Cambridge, Mass.: Harvard University Press, 1992).

[4]See David G. Herrmann, *The Arming of Europe and the Making of the First World War* (Princeton N.J.: Princeton University Press, 1996). There are a number of classic studies of the origins of World War I. These include Laurence Lafore, *The Long Fuse: An Interpretation of the Origins of the First World War* (1971; repr., Prospect Heights, Ill.: Waveland Press, 1997); James Joll, *The Origins of the First World War* (London: Longman, 1984); and R. J. W. Evans et al., eds., *The Coming of the First World War* (Oxford, U.K.: Clarendon Press, 1988). The interpretation above relies particularly on Hew Strachan, *The First World War*, vol. 1, *To Arms* (Oxford, U.K.: Oxford University Press, 2001).

[5]See Isabel V. Hull, *Absolute Destruction: Military Culture and the Practices of War in Imperial Germany* (Ithaca, N.Y.: Cornell University Press, 2005), for accounts of the military conduct in German Southwest Africa and the legacies of this. For a summation of the British in Africa, including the Boer War, see Philippa Levine, *The British Empire: From Sunrise to Sunset* (Harlow, U.K.: Pearson, 2007), and Peter Warwick, ed., *The South African War: The Anglo-Boer War, 1899–1902* (London: Longman, 1980).

[6]Charles Mangin, *La Force Noire* (Paris: Hachette, 1910), 346–48. For an assessment of Mangin, see Michael S. Neiberg, *Fighting the Great War: A Global History* (Cambridge, Mass.: Harvard University Press, 2005), 170.

[7]David Fromkin, *A Peace to End All Peace: The Fall of the Ottoman Empire and the Creation of the Modern Middle East* (New York: Henry Holt, 1989).

[8]John H. Morrow Jr., *The Great War: An Imperial History* (London: Routledge, 2005), 35–36.

[9]See Strachan, *The First World War* (2001), 1:56–57.

[10]There were a number of self-proclaimed and self-consciously avant-garde movements across Europe similarly fascinated by violence and by the desire to shock their elders.

[11]Strachan, *The First World War* (2001), 1:141.

[12]An overview of many of these works can be found in I. F. Clarke, *Voices Prophesying War: Future Wars, 1763–3749*, 2nd ed. (Oxford, U.K.: Oxford University Press, 1992).

[13]On prewar European pacifism, see Sandi E. Cooper, *Patriotic Pacifism: Waging War in Europe, 1815–1914* (New York: Oxford University Press, 1991).

[14]These details are the standard account of these events, found in Strachan, *The First World War* (2001), vol. 1, and summarized in Samuel R. Williamson Jr. and Russel Van Wyk, *July 1914: Soldiers, Statesmen, and the Coming of the Great War: A Brief Documentary History* (Boston: Bedford/St. Martin's, 2003).

[15]Jeffrey Verhey, *The Spirit of 1914: Militarism, Myth and Mobilization in Germany* (Cambridge, U.K.: Cambridge University Press, 2000); Peter Fritzsche, *Germans into Nazis* (Cambridge, Mass.: Harvard University Press, 1998); Strachan, *The First World War* (2001), vol. 1.

[16]Strachan, *The First World War* (2001), 1:150.

[17]Susan Pedersen, *Family, Dependence, and the Origins of the Welfare State: Britain and France, 1914–1945* (Cambridge, U.K.: Cambridge University Press, 1993), chap. 2.

[18]For a summary of these measures, see Susan R. Grayzel, *Women and the First World War* (Harlow, U.K.: Longman, 2002), 22–26.

[19]Strachan, *The First World War* (2001), vol. 1, chap. 10.

[20]See ibid., 1:115–123, and Morrow, *The Great War*, 91–95.

[21]Morrow, *The Great War*, 89. See also Richard G. Hovannisian, ed., *Remembrance and Denial: The Case of the Armenian Genocide* (Detroit: Wayne State University Press, 1998).

[22]Alon Rachamimov, *POWs and the Great War: Captivity on the Eastern Front* (Oxford, U.K.: Berg, 2002), 3–4, 224–28.

[23]Tammy Proctor, *Female Intelligence: Women and Espionage in the First World War* (New York: New York University Press, 2003). On Mata Hari, see, among others, Julie Wheelwright, *The Fatal Lover: Mata Hari and the Myth of Women in Espionage* (London: Trafalgar Square, 1992).

[24]Maureen Healy, *Vienna and the Fall of the Habsburg Empire: Total War and Everyday Life in World War I* (Cambridge, U.K.: Cambridge University Press, 2004), 4–5; Peter Gatrell, *A Whole Empire Walking: Refugees in Russia during World War I* (Bloomington: Indiana University Press, 2005), 3; Stéphane Audoin-Rouzeau and Annette Becker, *14–18: Understanding the Great War*, trans. Catherine Temerson (New York: Hill & Wang, 2002), 85.

[25]For a discussion of the Bryce Committee's report and reception, see Nicoletta F. Gullace, *"The Blood of Our Sons": Men, Women, and the Renegotiation of British Citizenship during the Great War* (Houndmills, U.K.: Palgrave Macmillan, 2002), 17–33.

[26]See Paul G. Halpern, "The War at Sea," in *World War I: A History*, ed. Hew Strachan, 104–18 (Oxford, U.K.: Oxford University Press, 1998).

[27]Neiberg, *Fighting the Great War*, 175–76.

[28]John H. Morrow Jr., "The War in the Air," in *World War I: A History*, ed. Hew Strachan, 265–77 (Oxford, U.K.: Oxford University Press, 1998); Susan R. Grayzel, "The Souls of Soldiers: Civilians Under Fire in First World War France," *Journal of Modern History* 78 (2006): 588–622.

[29]On the radicalization of food protests, see Belinda Davis, *Home Fires Burning: Food, Politics, and Everyday Life in World War I Berlin* (Chapel Hill: University of North Carolina Press, 2000). For a useful summation of food supply policies, see Ian F. W. Beckett, *The Great War, 1914–1918* (Harlow, U.K.: Longman, 2001), 265–72.

[30]Philip J. Haythornthwaite, *The World War One Sourcebook* (London: Arms and Armour, 1992), 380–88.

[31]See Thomas C. Kennedy, *The Hound of Conscience: A History of the No-Conscription Fellowship, 1914–1919* (Fayetteville: University of Arkansas Press, 1981).

[32]See Regulation 40D, cited in Grayzel, *Women and the First World War*, 143.

[33]Grayzel, *Women and the First World War*, chap. 3 and chap. 5.

[34]Strachan, *The First World War* (2001), 1:497.

[35]See Morrow, *The Great War.*

[36]David Killingray, "The War in Africa," in *World War I: A History,* ed. Strachan, 92–97 (Oxford: Oxford University Press, 1998). See also Morrow, *The Great War,* 58–60, 96–100, 144–47, 200–2, and Hew Strachan, *The First World War* (New York: Simon & Schuster, 2003), 80–95.

[37]Strachan, *The First World War* (2003), 71–73.

[38]See Neiberg, *Fighting the Great War,* 168, and Morrow, *The Great War,* 129. Alistair Horne, *The Price of Glory: Verdun, 1916* (Harmondsworth, U.K.: Penguin, 1978), remains a definitive narrative account.

[39]Hew Strachan, *The First World War* (Harmondsworth, U.K.: Penguin, 2003), 192.

[40]For an overview of this day, see Martin Middlebrook, *The First Day on the Somme, 1 July 1916* (New York: W. W. Norton, 1972).

[41]Strachan, *The First World War* (2003), 193.

[42]See Keith Jeffery, *Ireland and the Great War* (Cambridge: Cambridge University Press, 2000), and Adrian Gregory and Senia Paseta, eds., *Ireland and the Great War: "A War to Unite Us All"?* (Manchester, U.K.: Manchester University Press, 2002).

[43]Neiberg, *Fighting the Great War,* 184–87.

[44]Ian F. W. Beckett, *The First World War* (Harlow, U.K.: Longman, 2001), 223. See also Leonard V. Smith, *Between Mutiny and Obedience* (Princeton, N.J.: Princeton University Press, 1994).

[45]Strachan, *The First World War* (2003), 252–53.

[46]Ibid., 257–58. See also Neiberg, *Fighting the Great War,* 272–75.

[47]Strachan, *The First World War* (2003), 229–30.

[48]On Berlin, see Davis, *Home Fires Burning.* On Vienna, see Healy, *Vienna and the Fall of the Habsburg Empire.*

[49]See a brief overview of some of the postwar violence in John Merriman, *A History of Modern Europe* (New York: W. W. Norton, 1996), 1140–42.

[50]Margaret MacMillan, *Paris 1919: Six Months That Changed the World* (New York: Random House, 2001).

[51]Ibid.

[52]Martin Kitchen, *Europe between the Wars* (Harlow, U.K.: Longman, 1988), 16.

[53]Eric Hobsbawm, *The Age of Extremes* (New York: Pantheon, 1994), 51.

[54]Fromkin, *A Peace to End All Peace,* 299.

[55]For more details, see ibid.

[56]MacMillan, *Paris 1919,* 98–106.

[57]See Richard J. Evans, *The Feminists: Women's Emancipation Movements in Europe, America, and Australasia, 1840–1920* (London: Croom Helm, 1977), for a comparison of women's suffrage. For France's failure, see Christine Bard, *Les filles de Marianne: Histoire des féminismes, 1914–1940* (Paris: Fayard, 1995).

[58]For more on this, see Gullace, *"The Blood of Our Sons,"* and Sandra Holton, *Feminism and Democracy: Women's Suffrage and Reform Politics in Britain, 1900–1918* (Cambridge, U.K.: Cambridge University Press, 1986).

[59]See a summary of these views in Grayzel, *Women and the First World War,* 101–11.

[60]Among the many significant studies of the cultural effects of the First World War, see Paul Fussell, *The Great War and Modern Memory* (Oxford, U.K.: Oxford University Press, 1975); Samuel Hynes, *A War Imagined: The First World War and English Culture* (New York: Atheneum, 1991); Modris Eksteins, *The Rites of Spring: The Great War and the Birth of the Modern Age* (Boston: Houghton Mifflin, 1989); and Vincent Sherry,

The Great War and the Language of Modernism (Oxford, U.K.: Oxford University Press, 2003).

[61] See Annette Becker, *Les monuments aux morts: Patrimoine et mémoire de la grande guerre* (Paris: Errance, 1988); Daniel J. Sherman, *The Construction of Memory in Interwar France* (Chicago: University of Chicago Press, 1999); and Jay Winter, *Sites of Memory, Sites of Mourning: The Great War in European Cultural History* (Cambridge, U.K.: Cambridge University Press, 1995).

PART TWO

The Documents

1

The Origins of the First World War

1

The Treaty of Vienna (The Dual Alliance)
1879

*The major European powers forged a variety of alliances in order to
secure their national and imperial interests in the decades leading up to
the First World War. In this brief excerpt from the treaty that helped set the
alliance system in motion, we can see how such diplomatic agreements
served to resolve arguments (such as the disputes over territory) and
solidify commitments among nations. The 1879 Treaty of Vienna created
the Dual Alliance between Germany and Austria-Hungary; it expanded
and became the Triple Alliance with the addition of Italy in 1882, an
arrangement that committed these states to one another's defense. A
less binding agreement between France and Russia, the Entente Cordiale (1904), broadened to become the Triple Entente, including Great
Britain, in 1907. This became possible only when Britain and Russia
resolved long-standing differences with the Anglo-Russian Entente the
same year. It is worth noting that the Dual Alliance, presented here,
specifically mentions that it aims to counter aggression by Russia. In
a similar fashion, when Italy joined the alliance, it declared that this
action should not be construed as antagonistic toward Britain. States
clearly wanted to band together to protect themselves against perceived
(and real) foes, but not to antagonize potential enemy states, at least not
overtly in the decades before 1914.*

From "The Treaty of Alliance between Germany and Austria, Vienna, October 7, 1879,"
in *The Great European Treaties of the Nineteenth Century*, ed. Augustus Oakes and R. B.
Mowat (Oxford, U.K.: Clarendon Press, 1921), 373.

Article I. If, contrary to expectation and against the sincere desire of both the High Contracting Parties, one of the two Empires shall be attacked on the part of Russia, the High Contracting Parties are bound to assist each other with the whole of the military power of their Empire, and consequently only to conclude peace conjointly and by agreement.

Article II. Should one of the High Contracting Parties be attacked by another Power, the other High Contracting Party hereby engages not only not to assist the aggressor against his High Ally, but at the least to observe a benevolent neutral attitude with regard to the High Contracting Party.

If, however, in such a case the attacking Power should be supported on the part of Russia, whether by way of active co-operation, or by military measures which menace the attacked Power, then the obligation of reciprocal assistance with full military power, which is stipulated in the first article of this Treaty, will in this case enter immediately into effect, and the conduct of war of both the High Contracting Parties shall be then also in common until the joint conclusion of Peace.

Article III. This Treaty, in conformity with its pacific character and to prevent any misconstruction, shall be kept secret by both High Contracting Parties, and it will be communicated to a Third Power only with the consent of both Parties, and strictly according to a special agreement.

2

The Hague Conventions
1907

In the thirty years before the outbreak of World War I, European states became more militarily and politically entangled through the alliance system. Perhaps paradoxically, they also sought to mitigate the potential dangers of a widespread pan-European or even larger conflict. The major global powers (including Russia, Germany, France, Austria-Hungary, Great Britain, the Ottoman Empire, and Japan) thus gathered twice in the decades before 1914 to negotiate restrictions on warfare. These states reached two sets of agreements, the Hague Conventions of 1899 and 1907. The excerpts from the 1907 conventions that follow detail efforts to contain existing abuses in older methods of warfare, particularly by spelling out procedures for the humane treatment of prisoners of war and restrictions on the "means of injuring the enemy." One key aspect of the 1907 agreement was that although naval attacks on undefended, or "open," locations—such as ports serving a military purpose—were allowed, aerial attacks (still more imaginary than real as shown in Document 4) were not.

Section I.—On Belligerents

CHAPTER II.—PRISONERS OF WAR

Article 4.   Prisoners of war are in the power of the hostile Government, but not in that of the individuals or corps who captured them.

They must be humanely treated. . . .

Article 5.   Prisoners of war may be interned in a town, fortress, camp, or other place, under obligation not to go beyond certain fixed limits;

From James Brown Scott, ed., *The Hague Conventions and Declarations of 1899 and 1907*, 3rd ed. (New York: Oxford University Press, 1918), 623–27.

but they can only be placed in confinement as an indispensable measure of safety, and only while the circumstances which necessitate the measure continue to exist. . . .

Article 7.   The Government into whose hands prisoners of war have fallen is charged with their maintenance.

In the absence of a special agreement between the belligerents, prisoners of war shall be treated as regards food, quarters, and clothing, on the same footing as the troops of the Government which has captured them.

Article 8.   Prisoners of war shall be subject to the laws, regulations, and orders in force in the army of the State in whose power they are. Any act of insubordination justifies the adoption towards them of such measures of severity as may be necessary.

Escaped prisoners who are retaken before being able to rejoin their army or before leaving the territory occupied by the army that captured them are liable to disciplinary punishment.

Prisoners who, after succeeding in escaping, are again taken prisoners, are not liable to any punishment for the previous flight.

Article 9.   Every prisoner of war is bound to give, if questioned on the subject, his true name and rank, and if he infringes this rule, he is liable to a curtailment of the advantages accorded to the prisoners of war of his class. . . .

Article 13.   Individuals who follow an army without directly belonging to it, such as newspaper correspondents and reporters, sutlers and contractors, who fall into the enemy's hands, and whom the latter thinks fit to detain, are entitled to be treated as prisoners of war, provided they are in possession of a certificate from the military authorities of the army they were accompanying. . . .

Article 18.   Prisoners of war shall enjoy complete liberty in the exercise of their religion, including attendance at the services of whatever church they may belong to, on the sole condition that they comply with the measures of order and police issued by the military authorities. . . .

Article 20.   After the conclusion of peace, the repatriation of prisoners of war shall be carried out as quickly as possible.

Section II. — On Hostilities

CHAPTER I. — MEANS OF INJURING THE ENEMY, SIEGES,
AND BOMBARDMENTS

Article 22. The right of belligerents to adopt means of injuring the enemy is not unlimited.

Article 23. In addition to the prohibitions provided by special Conventions, it is especially forbidden:

(*a*) To employ poison or poisoned weapons;

(*b*) To kill or wound treacherously individuals belonging to the hostile nation or army;

(*c*) To kill or wound an enemy who, having laid down his arms, or having no longer means of defense, has surrendered at discretion;

(*d*) To declare that no quarter will be given;

(*e*) To employ arms, projectiles, or material calculated to cause unnecessary suffering;

(*f*) To make improper use of a flag of truce, of the national flag or of the military insignia and uniform of the enemy . . . ;

(*g*) To destroy or seize the enemy's property, unless such destruction or seizure be imperatively demanded by the necessities of war;

(*h*) To declare abolished, suspended, or inadmissible in a court of law the rights and actions of the nationals of the hostile party.

It is likewise forbidden a belligerent to force the nationals of the hostile party to take part in the operations of war directed against their country, even if they were in its service before the commencement of the war.

Article 24. Ruses of war and the employment of measures necessary for obtaining information about the enemy and the country are considered permissible.

Article 25. It is forbidden to attack or bombard, by any means whatever, towns, villages, dwellings or buildings that are not defended.

3

BERTHA VON SUTTNER

Lay Down Your Arms

1889

---

*The voicing of antiwar attitudes in literature helped foster the climate
in which efforts to curtail war, such as the Hague Conventions (Document 2), emerged. This can be seen in the popular and widely translated
novel by Baroness Bertha von Suttner (1843–1914) called* Die Waffen
Nieder, *or* Lay Down Your Arms. *An Austrian who was descended from
both aristocratic and military families, Suttner spent the second half of
her life conducting vociferous campaigns for peace and disarmament
that culminated in her winning the Nobel Peace Prize in 1905. She died
on June 21, 1914, active until the end in preparing for the Twenty-First
Universal Peace Congress scheduled to be held in Vienna that year, an
event that never took place. Her fictionalized account of her own life tells
the story of a wife and mother living through the wars of the nineteenth
century and criticizes war's glory and necessity. In the following excerpt,
the long-suffering female protagonist and narrator reflects on the aftermath of her beloved husband's death during the Franco-Prussian War
(1870–1871).*

Every night, and it must be at the same hour, I wake with an indescribable feeling of pain. My heart contracts painfully, and I feel as if forced
to weep bitter tears and utter sighs of agony. This lasts a few seconds,
without my awakened self quite knowing why the other unhappy self
is so unhappy. The next stage after this is a compassion embracing the
whole world, and a sigh, full of the most painful pity: "Oh you poor, poor
men!" And then I see next shrieking shapes which are being torn to
pieces by a rain of murderous shot, and then I recollect that my dearest
love too was so torn in pieces. . . .

I have never put off my mourning, not even at my son's wedding.
When any one has loved, possessed, and lost such a husband, and lost
him as I did, her love "must be stronger than death," her passion for

---

From Bertha von Suttner, *Lay Down Your Arms*, trans. T. Holmes, 2nd ed. (London:
Longmans, Green, 1914), 422–23.

vengeance can never cool. But whom does this anger threaten? On whom would I execute vengeance? The men who did the deed were not in fault. The only guilty party is the *spirit of war*, and it is on this that my work of persecution, all too weak as it is, must be exercised.

My son Rudolf agrees with my views, though this of course does not prevent him from going through his military exercises every year, and could not prevent him, either, from marching to the frontier, if the European war, which is always hanging over our heads, should break out. And then, perhaps, I shall have once more to see how all that is dearest to me in the world has to be sacrificed . . . , how a hearth blessed with love . . . has to be laid in ruins. Shall I have to see all this once more, and then once more to fall into irrecoverable madness, or shall I yet behold the triumph of justice and humanity, which now, at this very moment, is striving for accomplishment in widely extended associations and in all strata of society?

4

H. G. WELLS

The War in the Air

1908

At the same time that some Europeans were hoping to avert future war or at least make its conditions more humane, innovations in technology led others to speculate on what a future international conflict might bring. Many writers anticipated the horrors of these new forms of warfare in their fiction. Here the British author and visionary H. G. Wells (1866–1946) depicts the devastation that an aerial war might cause. Like the novels of Bertha von Suttner (Document 3), his works were translated into many languages. The war that broke out six years later involved airpower in a way that was eerily reminiscent of what Wells had envisaged, even though the scale of the destruction wrought by aerial attacks turned out to be less than he had feared.

From H. G. Wells, *The War in the Air* (New York: Macmillan, 1908), 249–53.

The special peculiarities of aerial warfare were of such a nature as to trend, once it had begun, almost inevitably towards social disorganisation. The first of these peculiarities was brought home to the Germans in their attack upon New York; the immense power of destruction an airship has over the thing below, and its relative inability to occupy or police or guard or garrison a surrendered position. Necessarily, in the face of urban populations in a state of economic disorganisation and infuriated and starving, this led to violent and destructive collisions, and even where the air-fleet floated inactive above, there would be civil conflict and passionate disorder below. Nothing comparable to this state of affairs had been known in the previous history of warfare, unless we take such a case as that of a nineteenth century warship attacking some large savage or barbaric settlement, or one of those naval bombardments that disfigure the history of Great Britain in the late eighteenth century. Then, indeed, there had been cruelties and destruction that faintly foreshadowed the horrors of the aerial war. Moreover, before the twentieth century the world had had but one experience, and that a comparatively light one, in the Communist insurrection of Paris,[1] 1871, of the possibilities of a modern urban population under warlike stresses.

A second peculiarity of airship war as it first came to the world that also made for social collapse, was the ineffectiveness of the early airships against each other. Upon anything below they could rain explosives in the most deadly fashion, forts and ships and cities lay at their mercy, but unless they were prepared for a suicidal grapple they could do remarkably little mischief to each other. The armament of the huge German airships, big as the biggest mammoth liners afloat, was one machine gun that could easily have been packed up on a couple of mules. In addition, when it became evident that the air must be fought for, the air-sailors were provided with rifles with explosive bullets of oxygen or inflammable substance, but no airship at any time ever carried as much in the way of guns and armour as the smallest gunboat on the navy list had been accustomed to do. Consequently, when these monsters met in battle, they manœuvred for the upper place, or grappled and fought like junks, throwing grenades, fighting hand to hand in an entirely mediæval fashion. The risks of a collapse and fall on either side came near to balancing in every case the chances of victory. As a consequence, and after their first experiences of battle, one finds a growing tendency on the

---

[1]The Commune (1871) was a revolution that took place in Paris between March and May 1871 and was triggered by France's defeat in the Franco-Prussian war.

part of the air-fleet admirals to evade joining battle and to seek rather the moral advantage of a destructive counter attack. . . .

The third peculiarity of aerial warfare was that it was at once enormously destructive and entirely indecisive. It had this unique feature, that both sides lay open to punitive attack. In all previous forms of war, both by land and sea, the losing side was speedily unable to raid its antagonist's territory and the communications. One fought on a "front," and behind that front the winner's supplies and resources, his towns and factories and capital, the peace of his country, were secure. If the war was a naval one, you destroyed your enemy's battle fleet and then blockaded his ports, secured his coaling stations, and hunted down any stray cruisers that threatened your ports of commerce. But to blockade and watch a coastline is one thing, to blockade and watch the whole surface of a country is another, and cruisers and privateers are things that take long to make, that cannot be packed up and hidden and carried unostentatiously from point to point. In aerial war the stronger side, even supposing it destroyed the main battle fleet of the weaker, had then either to patrol and watch or destroy every possible point at which he might produce another and perhaps a novel and more deadly form of flyer. It meant darkening his air with airships. It meant building them by the thousand and making aeronauts by the hundred thousand. A small uninflated airship could be hidden in a railway shed, in a village street, in a wood; a flying machine is even less conspicuous.

And in the air are no streets, no channels, no point where one can say of an antagonist, "If he wants to reach my capital he must come by here." In the air all directions lead everywhere.

Consequently it was impossible to end a war by any of the established methods. A, having outnumbered and overwhelmed B, hovers, a thousand airships strong, over his capital, threatening to bombard it unless B submits. B replies by wireless telegraphy that he is now in the act of bombarding the chief manufacturing city of A by means of three raider airships. A denounces B's raiders as pirates and so forth, bombards B's capital, and sets off to hunt down B's airships, while B, in a state of passionate emotion and heroic unconquerableness, sets to work amidst his ruins, making fresh airships and explosives for the benefit of A. The war became perforce a universal guerilla war, a war inextricably involving civilians and homes and all the apparatus of social life.

5

F. T. MARINETTI

Manifesto of Futurism

1909

Most Europeans had been spared the direct experience of warfare during the late nineteenth century. By the beginning of the twentieth century, writers such as the Italian innovator Filippo Tommaso Marinetti (1876–1944) hailed the prospect of war as an opportunity to reawaken the sleeping manhood of the continent. Many European states had instituted conscription, making military training a common male rite of passage, and modest numbers of troops engaged in overseas wars of empire. But for some Europeans, the glory and invigorating aspects of war were easy to idealize because war's brutal costs remained so abstract. Marinetti and members of the artistic and political movement that he founded, Futurism, were among those who praised war as potentially both purifying and ennobling for European society, especially European men. In the eleven points of the 1909 Futurist manifesto, we can see the essential elements of a cultural climate in which the changes brought by the new century might lead people to embrace speed, danger, and violence.

1. We intend to sing the love of danger, the habit of energy and fearlessness.

2. Courage, audacity, and revolt will be essential elements of our poetry.

3. Up to now literature has exalted a pensive immobility, ecstasy, and sleep. We intend to exalt aggressive action, a feverish insomnia, the racer's stride, the mortal leap, the punch and the slap.

4. We say that the world's magnificence has been enriched by a new beauty; the beauty of speed. A racing car whose hood is adorned with

From F. T. Marinetti, "Manifesto of Futurism," in *Marinetti: Selected Writings*, ed. R. W. Flint, trans. R. W. Flint and Arthur A. Coppotelli (New York: Farrar, Straus and Giroux, 1971, 1972), 41–42.

great pipes, like serpents of explosive breath—a roaring car that seems to ride on grapeshot—is more beautiful than the *Victory of Samothrace*.

5. We want to hymn the man at the wheel, who hurls the lance of his spirit across the Earth, along the circle of its orbit.

6. The poet must spend himself with ardor, splendor, and generosity, to swell the enthusiastic fervor of the primordial elements.

7. Except in struggle, there is no more beauty. No work without an aggressive character can be a masterpiece. Poetry must be conceived as a violent attack on unknown forces, to reduce and prostrate them before man.

8. We stand on the last promontory of the centuries! . . . Why should we look back, when what we want is to break down the mysterious doors of the Impossible? Time and Space died yesterday. We already live in the absolute, because we have created eternal, omnipresent speed.

9. We will glorify war—the world's only hygiene—militarism, patriotism, the destructive gesture of freedom-bringers, beautiful ideas worth dying for, and scorn for woman.

10. We will destroy the museums, libraries, academies of every kind, will fight moralism, feminism, every opportunistic or utilitarian cowardice.

11. We will sing of great crowds excited by work, by pleasure, and by riot; we will sing of the multicolored, polyphonic tides of revolution in the modern capitals; we will sing of the vibrant nightly fervor of arsenals and shipyards blazing with violent electric moons; greedy railway stations that devour smoke-plumed serpents; factories hung on clouds by the crooked lines of their smoke; bridges that stride the rivers like giant gymnasts, flashing in the sun with a glitter of knives; adventurous steamers that sniff the horizon; deep-chested locomotives whose wheels paw the tracks like the hooves of enormous steel horses bridled by tubing; and the sleek flight of planes whose propellers chatter in the wind like banners and seem to cheer like an enthusiastic crowd.

6

CHARLES MANGIN

The Black Force

1910

While some Europeans, such as the Futurists (Document 5), welcomed the idea of war, others plotted how their imperial nations could best succeed in a war to come. It was a sign of the increased significance of late-nineteenth-century New Imperialism — a movement that fostered the rapid expansion of European colonial empires into Africa and the exercising of more direct control over such territories — that military planners began to consider the use of colonized subjects as troops, even in intra-European conflicts. At the turn of the century, some military strategists took into account the benefits of both colonial labor and colonial troops to help an imperial power subdue the colonies and perhaps ultimately win a war against another imperial state. The French, in particular, developed units of colonial soldiers called tirailleurs. *In this excerpt from* La Force Noire *(The Black Force), published in 1910, French military officer Charles Mangin (1866–1925), one of several prewar strategists to publish treatises on the use of colonial troops, explained the advantages for France of making use of soldiers from its colonies in sub-Saharan Africa.*

The organizing of black troops has for its immediate goal maintaining our current effectiveness, which has been compromised by the decline of the French birthrate; it allows us to add to our regiments of Algerian tirailleurs, which will cooperate with the same goal, and achieve the complete utilization of our Arab and Berber resources. . . .

Very useful yesterday, necessary today, and indispensable tomorrow, black troops will not only give us numbers; they are composed of natural soldiers, accustomed to all deprivations and all dangers . . . ; they have precisely the qualities that the long struggles of modern war require: simplicity, endurance, tenacity, the instinct for combat, the absence of

From Charles Mangin, *La Force Noire* (Paris: Hachette, 1910), 342–43. Translated by Susan R. Grayzel, 2010.

nervousness, and the incomparable strength to face shock. Their arrival on the field of battle will produce a considerable moral effect against an adversary.

These precious advantages of number and of quality are some important factors . . . but if the fighting is drawn out, our African forces will constitute for us an almost indefinite reserve out of our adversary's reach and who will allow us to continue the fight until we have obtained a first success, and, once this success is obtained, to pursue the fight up to the final triumph.

2
Living through the First World War

Poetic Responses to the Outbreak of War

7

RUPERT BROOKE

Peace
1915

*Combatants and noncombatants, men and women alike, recognized that
something potentially life altering had arrived with the outbreak of war.
One of the ways in which they attempted to convey this sense of change
came through poems that offer compelling encapsulations of the war experience across national, geographic, and gender boundaries. Perhaps there
is no more famous presentation of the spirit of what came to be called
"war enthusiasm" than a poem penned by Rupert Brooke (1887–1915),
an acclaimed British writer, who enlisted in the Royal Navy and died of
blood poisoning in 1915 while en route to Gallipoli. His sonnet "Peace"
was published in the widely read volume* 1914 and Other Poems *in
1915.*

Now, God be thanked Who has matched us with His hour,
    And caught our youth, and wakened us from sleeping,
With hand made sure, clear eye, and sharpened power,
    To turn, as swimmers into cleanness leaping,

Rupert Brooke, "Peace," in *1914 and Other Poems* (London: Sidwick & Jackson, 1915), 66.

Glad from a world grown old and cold and weary,
  Leave the sick hearts that honour could not move,
And half-men, and their dirty songs and dreary,
  And all the little emptiness of love!

Oh! we, who have known shame, we have found release there,
  Where there's no ill, no grief, but sleep has mending,
    Naught broken save this body, lost but breath;
Nothing to shake the laughing heart's long peace there
  But only agony, and that has ending;
    And the worst friend and enemy is but Death.

8

ANNA AKHMATOVA

July 1914

1917

In stark contrast to Rupert Brooke's embracing of war and the opportunities that it provided for young men (Document 7), the Russian poet Anna Akhmatova (the pseudonym of Anna Andreyevna Gorenko, 1889–1966) offered a far more pessimistic and fearful perspective of the war at its outset. At odds with her government after the Russian Revolution of 1917, Akhmatova remained in the Soviet Union and chronicled the devastating impact of both world wars. Although "July 1914" appeared in her third volume of poetry, The White Flock, *in 1917, she dated its composition as "July 29, 1914." Akhmatova's poem uses images of blood, destruction, and loss that offer an especially potent evocation of full-scale war.*

Anna Akhmatova, "July 1914," from *The White Flock (Bella Staya) 1917*, trans. John Henriksen.

1

There's a burning smell. Four weeks
the dry peat's been burning in the bogs.
Even the birds haven't sung today,
the aspen no longer shivers.

The sun's become disfavored by God,
since Easter no rain sprinkles the fields.
A one-legged passerby came through
and, alone in the courtyard, said:

"Horrible times are near. Soon
we'll be crowded with fresh graves.
Expect famine, tremors, death all around,
eclipsing of the heaven's lights.

Except the enemy won't divide
our land as easily as that:
the Mother of God will unfurl her white
folds over our great griefs."

2

A sweet fragrance of juniper
floats from the burning woods.
For their soldier boys the wives are wailing,
widows' moans ring through the fields.

Not in vain were the public prayers,
O how the earth yearned for rain!
With red liquid the trampled fields
were warmly watered.

Low, low the empty sky,
and a voice is softly praying:
"They wound Your holy body,
they gamble for Your robes."

9

BRITISH RECRUITMENT POSTER

Women of Britain Say— "Go!"

1915

Propaganda in its modern form came into existence with the First World War. Participant nations created new branches of government authorized to control, produce, and regulate information about the national war effort. In some countries, notably Great Britain, which did not have a conscript military, the government used propaganda, including posters, to recruit men to join the war effort. Such images and their forthright words turned the complex motives for the war into simple and, it was hoped, persuasive ones. Many recruiting posters addressed both men and women, including this early example authorized by the British government's Parliamentary Recruiting Committee. "Women of Britain Say—'Go!'" appeals directly to both noncombatant women and potential male combatants. It depicts those at home asking their men to help protect them and preserve a presumably threatened way of life.

E. V. Kealey, 1915, Department of Art, Imperial War Museum, London.

10

GERMAN WAR BOND POSTER

*Help Us Triumph!**

1917

As the war continued, all states used visual images to help raise funds through war loans or to help support charitable efforts to aid the victims of war, including wounded soldiers. Illustrations featuring combatants often accompanied direct pleas for aid both moral and material. Directly addressing the viewer, the German soldier in this appeal asks the presumably noncombatant audience to "help us triumph" by supporting the national war loan. The poster implies that such aid will make the person supporting the war effort part of the "us" who will be victorious. It is worth noting that the soldier is wearing the emblems of modern warfare such as the gas mask around his neck.

---

*Translation of text: The slogan at the top of the poster reads "Help Us Triumph!" The writing at the bottom reads "Subscribe to the War Loan."

Fritz Erler, 1917, Hoover Institute Library, Stanford, Calif.

Helft uns siegen!

zeichnet
die
Kriegsanleihe

GERMAN WAR BOND POSTER

*Help Us Triumph!**

1917

As the war continued, all states used visual images to help raise funds through war loans or to help support charitable efforts to aid the victims of war, including wounded soldiers. Illustrations featuring combatants often accompanied direct pleas for aid both moral and material. Directly addressing the viewer, the German soldier in this appeal asks the presumably noncombatant audience to "help us triumph" by supporting the national war loan. The poster implies that such aid will make the person supporting the war effort part of the "us" who will be victorious. It is worth noting that the soldier is wearing the emblems of modern warfare such as the gas mask around his neck.

---

*Translation of text: The slogan at the top of the poster reads "Help Us Triumph!" The writing at the bottom reads "Subscribe to the War Loan."

Fritz Erler, 1917, Hoover Institute Library, Stanford, Calif.

11

RUSSIAN WAR BOND POSTER

*Freedom Loan**

1917

In this Russian poster, a soldier calls on a skeptical and increasingly impoverished population for financial support to continue the war effort of the failing Provisional Government after the first Russian Revolution. In the background of the poster, the messages urging the viewer not to let the "enemy take away the freedom that you have won" and "Freedom" suggest both that the war has helped to "free" Russia and that such liberation might be lost if Russia does not pursue war until victory.

*Translation of text: The writing on the top of the poster reads "Freedom Loan." The flags include the following slogans: far left, "War until victory"; second from left, "Victory over the enemy"; second from right, "Do not let the enemy take away the freedom that you have won"; and far right, "Freedom."

M. B. Kustodiev, 1917, Hoover Institute Library, Stanford, Calif.

12

FRENCH WAR BOND POSTER

Subscribe to the National War Loan*

1917

States continued to ask their civilian populations for monetary as well as moral support for the war. In Georges Redon's image for a French war loan poster in 1917, a mother getting ready to tuck her child into bed beneath the absent soldier-father's portrait underscores the poignancy of the appeal. Representing all long-suffering civilians who relied on and missed soldiers fighting at the front, the wife/mother—that emblem of the civilian—asks for financial aid to prevent all children from continuing to experience the "horrors of war." To underscore the specific French grievances that justified the conflict, a doll dressed in the traditional costume of Alsace is tucked into the girl's bed.

*Translation of text: "So that your children will no longer know the horrors of war, subscribe to the National War Loan, Société Générale [bank]."

Georges Redon, 1917, Hoover Institute Library, Stanford, Calif.

Pour que vos enfants ne connaissent plus les horreurs de la guerre,

SOUSCRIVEZ
À L'EMPRUNT NATIONAL
SOCIÉTÉ GÉNÉRALE

VISA N.º 9165   DEVAMBEZ IMP. PARIS.

Voices from the Battlefronts

13

JULIAN GRENFELL

Letter from a British Officer in the Trenches

November 18, 1914

Communication between soldiers and those they left behind was care-
fully managed. Belligerent states were understandably cautious about the
kinds of information those at the battlefront could provide to civilians.
And yet, despite extensive censorship, letters conveyed a great deal of the
emotional and physical experiences of war. The letter that follows was
reprinted in 1930 in a collection titled War Letters of Fallen Englishmen, *edited by critic, writer, and artist Laurence Housman. As Housman*
acknowledged, he benefitted in assembling the collection from educators
of the upper classes—reflected in the number of letters that came from
the officer class—and from the newly established Imperial War Museum.
Typical of the letters in this collection is this one by Captain the Hon-
orable Julian Grenfell describing trench warfare in its early stages in
November 1914. Grenfell was educated at Eton, perhaps the most elite
private school in Britain, and attended Oxford University before joining
the First Royal Dragoons. Nearly six months after writing this letter to his
parents, Grenfell died of wounds in France in May 1915. He was twenty-
seven years of age.

[FLANDERS]

[To His Parents:]   NOVEMBER 18TH, 1914
   . . . They had us out again for 48 hours [in the] trenches while I was
writing the above. About the shells, after a day of them, one's nerves
are really absolutely beat down. I can understand now why our infantry
have to retreat sometimes; a sight which came as a shock to me at first,

From Laurence Housman, ed., *War Letters of Fallen Englishmen* (London: E. P. Dutton,
1930), 119–20.

after being brought up in the belief that the English infantry cannot retreat.

These last two days we had quite a different kind of trench, in a dripping sodden wood, with the German trench in some places 40 yards ahead. . . . We had been worried by snipers all along, and I had always been asking for leave to go out and have a try myself. Well, on Tuesday the 16th, the day before yesterday, they gave me leave. Only after great difficulty. They told me to take a section with me, and I said I would sooner cut my throat and have done with it. So they let me go alone. Off I crawled through sodden clay and trenches, going about a yard a minute, and listening and looking as I thought it was not possible to look and to listen. I went out to the right of our lines, where the 10th were, and where the Germans were nearest. I took about 30 minutes to do 30 yards; then I saw the Hun trench, and I waited there a long time, but could see or hear nothing. It was about 10 yards from me. Then I heard some Germans talking, and saw one put his head up over some bushes, about 10 yards behind the trench. I could not get a shot at him, I was too low down, and of course I could not get up. So I crawled on again very slowly to the parapet of their trench. I peered through their loop-hole and saw nobody in the trench. Then the German behind me put up his head again. He was laughing and talking. I saw his teeth glistening against my foresight, and I pulled the trigger very slowly. He just grunted, and crumpled up. . . . I went out again in the afternoon in front of our bit of the line. I waited there for an hour, but saw nobody. . . . I reported the trench empty. The next day, just before dawn, I crawled out there again, and found it empty again. Then a single German came through the woods toward the trench. I saw him 50 yards off. He was coming along upright and careless, making a great noise. I heard him before I saw him. I let him get within 25 yards, and shot him in the heart. He never made a sound. Nothing for 10 minutes, and then there was a noise and talking, and a lot of them came along through the wood. . . . I counted about 20, and there were more coming. They halted in front, and I picked out the one I thought was the officer, or sergeant. He stood facing the other way, and I had a steady shot at him behind the shoulder. He went down, and that was all I saw. I went back at a sort of galloping crawl to our lines, and sent a message to the 10th that the Germans were moving up their way in some numbers. Half an hour afterwards, they attacked the 10th and our right, in massed formation, advancing slowly to within 10 yards of the trenches. We simply mowed them down. It was rather horrible.

14

HUGO MÜLLER

Letter from a German Soldier on the Western Front

October 17, 1915

This letter was reprinted in 1928 in Philipp Witkop's collection Kriegsbriefe gefallener Studenten, *an expanded version of two collections
edited and published during the war years. According to the introduction
to both the original edition and the condensed English translation, German Students' War Letters,* Witkop selected the missives in his book from
among 20,000 such letters placed in the hands of the German Ministry of
Education by relatives and friends of the slain men. The German edition
contained 131 letters, the English 95. This letter was written by Hugo
Müller, a law student from Leipzig, who was twenty-three years old when
he described conditions along the western front just south of Arras in
October 1915. His casual reference to the prospect of death and madness
and his astonishment at the humanity of the French enemy—who, like
him, wonders, "When will it all end?"—offer insight into the toll inflicted
on those waging this war. Müller died in October 1916.*

BEFORE AGNY, SOUTH-EAST OF ARRAS, OCTOBER 17TH, 1915.
I am enclosing a French field-postcard, which I want you to put with my
war-souvenirs. It came out of the letter-case of a dead French soldier. It
has been extremely interesting to study the contents of the letter-cases
of French killed and prisoners. The question frequently recurs, just as
it does with us: "When will it all end?" To my astonishment I practically
never found any expressions of hatred or abuse of Germany or German
soldiers. On the other hand, many letters from relations revealed an
absolute conviction of the justice of their cause, and sometimes also of
confidence in victory. In every letter mother, fiancée, children, friends,
whose photographs were often enclosed, spoke of a joyful return and
a speedy meeting—and now they are all lying dead and hardly even
buried between the trenches, while over them bullets and shells sing

From Philipp Witkop, ed., *German Students' War Letters*, trans. Annie F. Wedd (London:
Methuen, 1929), 278–79.

their gruesome dirge. Lucky the few whom we or those opposite have been able to inter with some sort of decency—for fragments of human bodies are still hanging in the barbed wire. Only a little while ago, close in front of our trench, was a human hand with a ring on one finger; a few yards away was a forearm, of which finally only the bone remained—so good does human flesh taste to rats! Ghastly! The man who could never shudder and shake would learn how here! I have learnt how *not* to do it! When at night I go all alone through the trenches and saps, and there is a rustling here and a rustling there, and at any moment *ein Neger*[1] may leap out at one's throat—all in the pitch-darkness—that really is gruesome; but I have gradually got used to it and have become as callous as our Landsturmers.[2] War hardens one's heart and blunts one's feelings, making a man indifferent to everything that formerly affected and moved him; but these qualities of hardness and indifference towards fate and death are necessary in the fierce battles to which trench-warfare leads. Anybody who allowed himself to realize the whole tragedy of some of the daily occurrences in our life here would either lose his reason or be forced to bolt across to the enemy's trench with his arms high in the air.

[1] A derogatory German term for black troops.
[2] Similar to a militia or reserve unit; a home guard.

15

CHRISTIAN CRESWELL CARVER

Letter from a British Officer Describing the Battle of the Somme

Late July 1916

Lieutenant Christian Carver was only nineteen years of age when he wrote to his younger brother Maurice about his experiences "fromewhere in Sanders" (somewhere in Flanders). Lieutenant Carver personified one type of British volunteer; he was educated at the elite prep school

From Laurence Housman, ed., *War Letters of Fallen Englishmen* (London: E. P. Dutton, 1930), 62–64.

Rugby and enlisted directly from the school. In other letters, he cautioned his brother to stay in England and complete his secondary education rather than join him along the western front. In this letter, he vividly but impressionistically describes the intensive bombardment that preceded the notorious Battle of the Somme, including the deafening impact of the guns, the sight of gas clouds (chemical weapons) rolling across the battle zone, and the confusion felt when facing a direct onslaught of artillery fire. Carver died on July 23, 1917, still somewhere in Flanders.

FROM EWHERE IN SANDERS.
SUNDAY MORN.
[LATE JULY, 1916]

[To a Brother]
Dear Maurice:
. . . Should this reach you, it will find you in camp, so that you will not read it, military operations very rightly coming first. . . . It is difficult to tell you about my personal experiences, as they are so bound up with technicalities. But one gets certain pictures absolutely engraved on one's soul.

The first is during the preliminary bombardment. Carroll and I stood on top of one of our gun pits one pitch-dark night, watching the show. Everything from 18 pdrs. to 15" appeared to be shooting. The familiar landscape showed up in fragments now here, now there, lighted by the blinding flash of the guns. A red glare and a shower of spark every ½ minute or so represented hun shrapnel on the Peronne road. Speech was of course impossible, and one could only stand and *feel* the thousands of tons of metal rushing away from one. Impressive enough, but what I shall never forget was a substratum of noise, an unceasing moaning roar, exactly like enormous waves on a beach. The 75's firing over Maricourt Wood, a shell passing over trees makes a noise exactly like a great wave. Or was it indeed the breakers of the Sea of Death beating against the harbour gates of the hun, beating until it swept them and him away, washed them back and threw them up, only to be washed further yet by the next tide. I think it was. The second is from Montauban valley, at dawn on the 6th July. Straight opposite was the as yet untaken Bazentin ridge,[1] beyond which we could just see the spires and roofs of the 2 Bazentins.[2] On the skyline High Wood. To the left, rising

[1] Battle of Bazentin Ridge, July 14–17, a subset of the Battle of the Somme.
[2] The 2 Bazentins refers to the two neighboring villages Bazentin-le-Grand and Bazentin-le-Petit (Large Bazentin and Small Bazentin).

out of the smoke and mist, the dark mass of Mametz Wood, beyond it Contalmaison. To the right—dawn. I shall never forget that either. Silhouetted against Mithras'[3] morning legions, all fiery red, and fierce gold, the dark sinister line of Longueval, houses, spires *now* all gone, showing among the trees of Delville Wood. And in an open space the incongruously complete buildings, and factory chimneys of Waterlot farm. Nearer the remains of Montaubon and Trones Wood.

The third is from the same place some hours later, when we looked down into hell on our left. A frontal attack on Contalmaison and Mametz Wood (quite different and separate from Mametz village) which we saw from our ridge to a flank. Every kind of shell bursting in the wood and village. Shrapnel, crump, incendiary, lachrymatory, and over the torn-up waste of what had once been trenches and over which our people had to advance, hun "Woolly bears" (5.9″ Shrapnel), crumps, and a steady barrage of field-gun shrapnel from Baz. Wood, fortunately bursting much too high. By way of a frame for this happy scene, one saw it through the hun flank barrage bursting on the brow of our hill about 200 yards in front of us. He put a barrage on us too, but as it was 25 yards behind us, and apparently meant to stop there, it soon ceased to worry us. Presently one saw great clouds of gas sweeping across, and I must say I felt we were looking into hell indeed. Then little black figures which formed into lines, which presently moved slowly forward. Gigantic shell[s] seemed to pitch right into the line, but they still went on, now disappearing into a trench, but ever moving on forward when they reappeared, their work accomplished. And so one lost sight of them in the welter of smoke, and only saw occasional little single figures (messengers) running steadfastly back across the plain. Sometimes a shell burst and one saw them no more. Carroll arrived to relieve me and we wended our perilous way down to the battery and breakfast.

The last impression is the morning of the 17th. We went along the Briqueterie road and round into our valley of the shadow. The great valley was already nearly ploughed from end to end, and here and there whizz-bangs were bursting. We got to our position, in a sort of little hollow, and the ordered confusion of getting into action was at its height when with a shriek and a crash a shell burst some 20 yards behind us. Then a bang—and the yell of the shell case as it went through us. I remember looking down the battery. The driver standing beside me was lying killed. A Gunner who was behind me got the bullet I should otherwise

---

[3]Mithras, the Roman god of Morning.

have had, in the stomach. A little further on someone was bending over Wager, and I saw Bowman crawling into the trench with his leg broken. Wounded men lying about, some dead horses. There is no hope of taking cover in a case like that, you just have to stand by your horses. Everybody behaved rippingly. I saw little Sparkie, my groom, unconcernedly holding my ponies. Well, old spot, be good if you can't be clever. Yrs.

C. C. CARVER

16

KARL GORZEL

Letter from a German Soldier on the Battle of the Somme

October 1, 1916

Karl Gorzel, born in 1895, was killed while fighting in March 1918. A nineteen-year-old law student when the war broke out, he describes here the aftermath of the Battle of the Somme from a German soldier's perspective. Like the letter by Hugo Müller (Document 14), this one was reprinted in 1928 in Philipp Witkop's collection Kriegsbriefe gefallener Studenten *(German Students' War Letters).*

OCTOBER 1ST, 1916 (AFTER THE BATTLE OF THE SOMME). Now that the horrible affair at Thiepval lies like a bad dream behind me, I will tell you in broad outline how I have been faring on the Somme. . . .

As we were passing through Cambrai we saw Hindenburg and greeted him with exultant cheers. The sight of him ran through our limbs like fire and filled us with boundless courage. We were going to feel the need of him too!

On the evening of September 11th we relieved the 5th Guards (Regulars) in the Thiepval position. The march up was awful. The

From Philipp Witkop, ed., *German Students' War Letters*, trans. Annie F. Wedd (London: Methuen, 1929), 372–74.

nearer we got, the more intense became the gun-fire and the flatter the communication-trenches, which at last disappeared altogether. Then we had to advance in spurts through the murderous shrapnel- and shell-fire. Even there we had heavy casualties.

The next morning the English attack began and the guns were not silent for two hours during the day. At dawn I looked around me: what a ghastly picture! Not a trace of a trench left; nothing but shell-holes as far as the eye could reach—holes which had been filled by fresh explosions, blown up again and again filled. In them we lay as flat on the ground as if we were dead, for already flocks of enemy aeroplanes were humming over us. We were absolutely at their mercy, and with remorse-less accuracy they directed the English heavy-guns, shell after shell, into our line, and themselves fired with machine-guns at everybody who made the slightest movement below.

Hour after hour passed. The wounded lie helplessly groaning. The supply of water runs out. The day seems to stretch itself maliciously to twice its usual length. The fire increases to such bewildering inten-sity that it is no longer possible to distinguish between the crashes. Our mouths and ears are full of earth; three times buried and three times dug up again, we wait—wait for night or the enemy! Oh that wait-ing!—it scorches the brain and drives one frantic. And the bursting shells' dance-of-death becomes ever madder—one can see nothing for smoke, fire, and spurting earth. Feverishly one's eyes seek to penetrate the curtain of fire and detect the advancing enemy.

Suddenly the barrage lifts—the shells are falling behind us—and there, close in front, is the first wave of the enemy! Release at last! Every one who is not wounded, every one who can raise an arm, is up, and like a shower of hailstones our bombs pelt upon the attacking foe! The first wave lies prone in front of our holes, and already the second is upon us, and behind the English are coming on in a dense mass. Anyone who reaches our line is at once polished off in a hand-to-hand bayonet fight, and now our bombs fly with redoubled force into the enemy's ranks. They do their gruesome work there, and like ripe ears of corn before the reaper the English attacking columns fall. Only a few escape in full flight back through the boyaux.[1]

We sink down, dazed, upon the tortured earth, and tie up the wounded as well as we can, while awaiting the coming of a second attack or of the night. The machine-guns are buried in soil and smashed by shells; the stock of bombs is almost exhausted; the fire becomes more violent

[1] Literally, a long and narrow passage; in this context of trench warfare, a communi-cation trench.

again; it makes one's head ache and one's lips burn. The issue lies now in the Hands of God. There is only one thought in every mind: "They shan't take us alive!" But the Tommies have had enough; they won't come back to-day. It gets darker and the fire becomes normal. I light a cigarette and try to think—to think of our dead and wounded; of the sufferings of humanity; to think back to—home! But away with such thoughts! The present demands its rights—it requires a real man, not a dreamer. Food arrives and drink—*drink*! The stretcher-bearers carry the wounded back as far as they can. Reinforcements arrive, things are cleared up and the dead buried, and a new day breaks, more horrible than the last!

Such is the battle of the Somme—Germany's bloody struggle for victory. This week represents the utmost limit of human endurance—it was hell!

17

SOWAR SOHAN SINGH

Letter from a Soldier in the British Indian Army
July 10, 1915

Colonial soldiers faced additional hardships during their military service. They were even more isolated by geography and language from their homes than their European counterparts. This letter comes from a collection assembled by historian David Omissi to provide access to the Indian experience of the war. All of the letters were found in government censorship files. Here Sowar Sohan Singh echoes the sentiments of other, more privileged, troops about the destruction and futility of the conflict.

KITCHENER'S INDIAN HOSPITAL   [URDU]
BRIGHTON   10TH JULY 1915
The state of things here is indescribable. There is a conflagration all around, and you must imagine it to be like a dry forest in a high wind in the hot weather, with abundance of dry grass and straw. No one can

From David Omissi, ed., *Indian Voices of the Great War: Soldiers' Letters, 1914–18* (New York: St. Martin's Press, 1999), 77.

extinguish it but God himself—man can do nothing. What more can I write? You must carefully consider what I say. Here thousands of lives have been sacrificed. Scratch the ground to a depth of one finger, and nothing but corpses will be visible. They say that God is the great and everlasting soul of the universe, and it is only a year since all these souls were seated amongst their friends and relations and enjoying all the delights of life, and now the whole of them are lying hidden under the ground.

18

BEHARI LAL

Letter from a Soldier in the British Indian Army

November 28, 1917

As was the case with soldiers everywhere, communication between colonial troops from India and their friends and family back home was tightly censored. We know very little about the writers of such letters, not even whether they were literate or dictated their words to a scribe (the more likely scenario). In this letter, Behari Lal complains about his treatment by the army. Unsurprisingly, the letter was not allowed to reach its intended recipient; government censors described his comments as "likely to do harm in India."

SUPPLY AND TRANSPORT CORPS
SECUNDERABAD CAVALRY BRIGADE   28TH NOVEMBER 1917
There is no likelihood of our getting rest during the winter. I am sure German prisoners would not be worse off in any way than we are. I had to go three nights without sleep, as I was on a motor lorry, and the lorry fellows, being Europeans, did not like to sleep with me, being an Indian. [The] cold was terrible, and it was raining hard; not being able to sleep on the ground in the open, I had to pass the whole night sitting on

From David Omissi, ed., *Indian Voices of the Great War: Soldiers' Letters, 1914–18* (New York: St. Martin's Press, 1999), 336–37.

the outward lorry seats. I am sorry the hatred between Europeans and Indians is increasing instead of decreasing, and I am sure the fault is not with the Indians. I am sorry to write this, which is not a hundredth part of what is in mind, but this increasing hatred and continued ill-treatment has compelled me to give you a hint.

19

MEHMEN ARIF ÖLÇEN

Memoir of a Turkish Prisoner of War
1917–1918

Given the arrangements agreed on under the prewar Hague Conventions (Document 2), prisoners of war could expect reasonable treatment during the First World War. While all combatants risked imprisonment if caught by the enemy, soldiers fighting on the eastern front had a much greater likelihood of being taken prisoner than in other theaters of the war. In addition to the frustration of imprisonment, POWs often had legitimate complaints about their living conditions. This memoir of a Turkish POW in Russia was composed after the war based on his notes and personal reflections. It provides a valuable glimpse of the experience of POWs and also of conditions in Russia in 1917.

In the distance, smoke was rising from the snow. There was probably a shelter, underground bunker, or cabin there. We went toward the place from which the smoke rose. The soldiers stopped before a bunker buried in the snow. Over the door was stretched a tent canvas. The soldiers motioned for me to enter. When I poked my head inside, two Russian officers looked at me. One of them was young. The other was about forty-five years old.

"*Pozhaluista* (Please)!" they said, wanting me to enter.

From Mehmen Arif Ölçen, *Vetluga Memoir: A Turkish Prisoner of War in Russia, 1916–1918*, ed. and trans. Gary Leiser (Gainesville: University Press of Florida, 1995), 38, 99–101.

I went inside. We looked at each other. I sat where they indicated. They did not understand what I said nor did I understand them. They summoned a soldier from Kazan. This soldier was going to translate.

"*Kakoy chin* (What is your rank)?" asked the older officer.

"*Poruchik.*"

"How old are you?"

"Twenty-three."

"Are you happy to be a prisoner?"

"No," I said. How could I be happy? This morning I was a company commander. Now I'm a prisoner.

"If a man's life were saved, wouldn't he be glad? At twenty-three, don't you want to enjoy life? We would certainly prefer to be prisoners if we could."

After saying this, the Russian officer turned to the man from Kazan and said, "Ask him who the soldiers are who are facing us! Turks or Kurds?"

I then understand that they especially feared the Kurds because the Kurds immediately killed any Russian whom they captured. I inferred from this that these two Russian officers wanted to be captured by Turks.

"The soldiers facing you are Turks," I answered.

The young Russian officer who appeared to be a lieutenant interrupted. "You captured this place and then we captured this place. Is there any sense in shedding each other's blood? Russia is a very large country. Even if it wins the war, will the captured lands be given to the Russian villagers? It will become part of the estates of the nobility from the czar's family. Russia is shedding blood for their pleasure. A great many officers think the way I do."

...A friendship began to develop, and they continued to speak frankly. There were other officers in the Russian army who thought like them. At the first opportunity on the front, they apparently wanted to go over to the Turkish side. They took from their pockets notebooks in which they had kept a daily record of events. Captured Turkish officers had written statements in these notebooks. The Russian officers had them read out and translated into Russian. One of the Turks had written, "I truly have great sorrow for the Russian officer who will lose his life to a bullet tomorrow." They wanted me to write something as well. I wrote the following: "When I was captured, I was treated with great kindness by this officer. If he is captured by our army, I hope my brothers-in-arms will protect him." They were pleased. Then I added, "A Turkish regiment is facing you. They surely will not fail to respect you." ...

In the barracks to which we were moved were sixty-two officers and fifteen enlisted men. They lodged five or six of us in a small, narrow room in the attic. Here we were to stay. There was no place to move in this building. Its courtyard was very narrow. One could not walk back and forth in it. The courtyard was surrounded by a wooden fence. The building itself was of timber and in a decrepit state. Directly across from it was the home of a Russian colonel, in two rooms of which were lodged six majors and a lieutenant colonel.

When the commander came for the evening inspection, we showed him the narrow room in the attic and said, "This is not a suitable place for prisoners. Is this the place where you said we would be comfortable?" He spoke somewhat apologetically and left.

In his place came our former arrogant commander who said in a very rude and harsh manner, "What can I do about it? The Germans have killed many of our prisoners. This is how we shall conduct ourselves for now." Later he read an order that had come from Moscow: "The prisoners will have two *funds* (a *fund* is about twelve ounces) of bread each day, one black and one white, one *fund* of sugar each month, and meat once every three days." After reading this, he left.

In this barracks, which now held more than ninety prisoners, there was no room for a man to step. A great many of us ate our meals while sitting on our beds. . . .

The severest part of the winter for us was the last week of January 1917. The temperature dropped to minus twenty degrees. A red flag was hung from the clock tower and official buildings. This was done when it was extremely cold to indicate that no one should go out and all offices and schools were closed. No one went into the street. The marketplace was deserted.

A thick sheet of ice covered all the windows. Some of us wrapped ourselves in our military cloaks. Others wrapped themselves in linen and lay in bed with only their mouths and noses exposed. The toilet was some distance away in a shed outside the barracks. It was impossible for anyone to go there. Even the Russians, who wore fur clothing and fur caps that covered their ears, did not go outside. . . .

It seemed that we would die of starvation. In the first week of February, another cold wave again imprisoned us in our rooms. Again a red flag was hung from the clock tower. The temperature dropped to minus thirty degrees. Once more the city sank into a deep silence. The stoves were full of burning wood, but we still shivered. Our stove was so cleverly constructed that when the wood burned it heated three rooms. This stove was called a *bez gari*. A separate pipe connected it to a hole near the ceiling. After the stove was filled with wood and it began to burn, this hole was closed. When the wood had turned completely to hot coals, the hole was opened and hot air circulated through the gaps between the walls of the rooms. Sometimes the heat was so great that it drove us outside. While the wood in the stove burned, the chimney hole was kept open. . . .

At the same time, we all seemed to be starving to death. The so-called meat that was given to the garrison was ox and water buffalo heads that had been preserved under the snow. They were covered with maggots. We boiled them in water and ate them. The odor upset our stomachs and made us vomit. The amount of bread was reduced to about six ounces a day. We made soup with cabbage leaves that had been finely sliced and sealed in earthenware jars in the summer for use in the winter. The smell of the soup was so bad, however, that we couldn't drink it.

20

LIDIIA ZAKHAROVA

Diary Entry from a Russian Nurse at the Battlefront

1915

Since the Crimean War (1853–1856) and the endeavors of Florence Nightingale, the role of the military nurse had become an acceptable and necessary one for nations waging war. It was one of the vital and widespread tasks undertaken by women across the war zones. In addition to ranks of professional nurses, the war called forth the labor of many women who would otherwise never have undertaken such difficult, bloody work. Young, middle-, and upper-class women in almost every participant state volunteered to take on tasks that required both menial labor and the emotional strength to deal with the mangled and dying bodies of young men. In the case of women like this Russian mother, Lidiia Zakharova,

From Lidiia Zakharova, "Diary of a Red Cross Sister in the Front-Lines," trans. Cynthia Simmons, in *Lines of Fire: Women Writers of World War I*, ed. Margaret R. Higonnet (New York: Plume, 1999), 184–85.

*service as a wartime nurse meant leaving her own children behind to
take care of other mothers' sons.*

That evening I saw the German trenches for the first time. I can't deny
it—our enemies were rather comfortably ensconced. Their trenches
were one great labyrinth, an entire complex system of underground cor-
ridors, nooks, dugouts, and blind alleys.

In the officers' dugouts the ground was covered with boards, some
floors even laid with rugs. Everywhere there were camp beds and col-
lapsible furniture stolen from those very estates that burned so quickly
and furiously, illuminating the land all around with a purple glow. On
the table—wine bottles, china, and crystal beside crude soldiers' mugs.
There were greasy plates with some scraps of food, corks, and cigarette
butts.

In one of the dugouts my attention was drawn to a discarded, toppled
child's high chair. The presence of this mute witness to the bloody epi-
sode that had just been played out was as disturbing as the presence of
the chair's little master would have been, and it made even more hor-
rifying and monstrous the sight of trenches overflowing with masses of
dead bodies.

It was a gruesome spectacle. A city of the dead, its inhabitants frozen
in the most unlikely positions, as if a raging, deadly hurricane had just
swept past. Some were lying on their backs, others face down. They were
all intertwined, so you could not tell whose arms and legs were whose.
Many were sitting in poses that made them seem alive, leaning on the
parapet or the back wall of the trench. But most terrible were those who
had not fallen, but stood shoulder to shoulder, still holding their rifles,
eyes open and glazed with the tranquility of non-existence, as if they
were listening to the ominous cries of the crows flying overhead.

There is a limit, by the way, beyond which the human mind can perceive no more horrors, as a saturated sponge can soak up no more
water. This thought was not original with me, but I remember I realized
its full meaning only at that time in the dugouts of the German trenches,
and I was astounded at how the person who pronounced it had truly
understood the capricious and multifaceted nature of human beings.

We simply went on with our work, neatly and efficiently, only rarely
exchanging a few necessary words.

"A stretcher."

"Help me, nurse, hold his head. . . ."

"Come here, please. . . ."
And again, "A stretcher . . ."
In one place we came across a strange group. A Russian and a German soldier caught in hand-to-hand combat had been killed on the spot by a shell exploding nearby. So they lay in each other's arms, recent enemies reconciled by the majesty of death. Evening fell. Low gray clouds crept over the field, once plowed up—now blown up by shells.

21

HENRI BARBUSSE

Under Fire

1916

Telling war stories offered combatants an opportunity to depict their experiences for a larger audience than letters allowed. Combatants from all the participant nations wrote thinly veiled depictions of their wartime experiences. Some were published to great acclaim during the war, such as Henri Barbusse's Le Feu *(Under Fire), which first appeared in France in 1916 and went on to win the prestigious Prix Goncourt. Barbusse (1873–1935) wrote the novel while recuperating from wounds that would cause him to be discharged from the army in 1917. His war experiences led him to pacifism, socialism, and communism; he ended up moving to the Soviet Union after the war. The following excerpt about facing battles such as that of Verdun in many ways reflects his politics, but when his book was translated into European languages, it also gained a following for its accurate depiction of wartime conditions.*

"Halt!"
An intense, furious, atrocious burst of gunfire was smashing against the parapets of the trench where they had just stopped us.
"Fritz is having a go. He's afraid of an attack, he's going crazy! What a go he's having!"

From Henri Barbusse, *Under Fire*, trans. Robin Buss (New York: Penguin, 2003), 201–3.

A dense hail of metal was pouring down on us, slicing its frightful way through the air, scratching and brushing across the plain.

I looked through a slit, and had this strange, brief vision:

Ahead of us, some ten metres away at most, there were motionless, outstretched bodies, one beside another, a row of soldiers, mown down; and, from every direction, clouds of bullets and shells were riddling this row of dead men with holes.

The bullets that swept across the ground in straight lines, raising little linear clouds, were holing and battering the bodies rigidly pinned to the ground, breaking the stiffened limbs, pounding into pale, empty faces, bursting liquefied eyeballs, splattering them around. Beneath the onslaught one could see the row of dead men move a little, shifting around in places. You could hear the dry noise made by the plunging dots of copper as they ripped through clothing and flesh: the sound of a ferocious knife or a noisy blow from a stick on clothes. Above us rushed a host of sharp whistling sounds, with the descending tone, always lower down the scale, of ricochets. We bent our heads beneath this extraordinary barrage of cries and voices.

"We've got to get out of the trench! Hurry!"

We leave this tiny corner of the battlefield where the gunfire is tearing, wounding and killing corpses all over again. We head right and to the rear. The communication trench goes uphill. At the top of the ravine, we pass in front of a telephone post and a group of artillery officers and gunners.

Here we halt once again. Kicking our heels we listen to the observer gunner shouting orders which the telephonist, buried beside him, picks up and relays.

"First gun, same height. Two tenths to the left. Three rounds a minute!"

A few of us have ventured to put our heads above the edge of the parapet and manage for a fraction of a second to take in the whole of the battlefield around which our company has been vaguely marching ever since this morning. I see a vast grey plain, across which the wind seems to be blowing light, mixed waves of dust broken at intervals by a sharper drift of smoke.

This huge expanse, across which the sun and the clouds spread patches of black and white, flashes here and there; those are our guns firing, and for a moment I saw it entirely sprinkled with brief bursts of fire. A moment later part of the countryside has been smothered in a blanket of whitish vapour, a kind of hurricane of snow.

In the distance, on the interminable and sinister fields, half concealed and the colour of rags, pitted with holes like a necropolis, you can see the slender skeleton of a church, like a piece of torn paper, and, from one side of the picture to the other, vague ranks of vertical marks, close together and underlined, like pages of schoolchildren's writing; these are tree-lined roads. Thin winding lines cross the plain backwards and forwards, chopping it up, and these lines are dotted with men.

You can see the fragments of lines formed by these human dots who, emerging from the depression, are moving over the plain beneath this frightful, savage sky.

It is hard to believe that each of these minute smudges is a being of flesh, trembling and fragile, infinitely vulnerable, but full of deep thoughts, full of long memories and full of a host of images. It is dazzling, this sprinkling of men as small as the stars in the sky.

My poor fellow men, poor unknown brothers, it is your turn for sacrifice. Another time it will be ours. Tomorrow, perhaps, it will be our turn to feel the skies bursting over our heads and the ground opening beneath our feet, to be assaulted by a prodigious army of missiles and to be swept aside by blasts a hundred thousand times more powerful than a hurricane.

They push us into the rear shelters. The field of death is extinguished from our eyes. In our ears, the thunder is deadened against the mighty anvil of the clouds. The noise of universal destruction falls still. Egotistically, the squad wraps itself in the familiar sounds of life and sinks into the caressing smallness of the shelters.

22

GINO CHARLES SPERANZA

Diary Entry from an American on the Italian Front

1917

After Italy entered the war in 1915, Italian American journalist and lawyer Gino Charles Speranza (1872–1927) traveled to Italy and worked as a correspondent for the New York Evening Post *and the weekly magazine* Outlook. *Once the United States joined the Allies two years later, he attached himself to the U.S. embassy in Rome, eventually serving as an assistant there. Throughout his time in Italy, Speranza kept a diary in which he recorded his impressions of the war. His widow, Florence Colgate Speranza, edited his wartime diary and published it in 1941. The hostile terrain of the Alps presented its own challenges to the Italian and Austro-Hungarian troops who faced one another across the vertical, snow-swept battlefield. In this excerpt from Speranza's diary, he details his visit to this site of battle, expressing his respect for the soldiers who fought under such difficult conditions and recording in a matter-of-fact way one of the brutal realities of the war: the transformation of an otherwise healthy man into a* mutilato—*a permanently disabled individual who had to return to postwar life minus an arm, a leg, or an eye. The postwar world was filled with such men.*

The Italian camp on Pizzo Serauta, a peak of the Marmolada, is between 9,000 to 10,000 feet high. The Alpini[1] reach it on foot in from six to eight and a half hours, according to the weather. It may be reached also in cages operating on three *teleferiche*[2] comprising the longest and most acute-angled system of wireways on the Italian front, in which passengers are hoisted 8,000 feet up from the starting point. . . . Up we went, . . . somewhat joltingly, with a disquieting, hesitating limp now and then,

---

[1]Specially trained mountain warfare soldiers in the Italian army.
[2]Cable ways.

From *The Diary of Gino Speranza: Italy, 1915–1919*, ed. Florence Colgate Speranza (New York: Columbia University Press, 1941), 2:74–76.

not in a cage . . . but in a wooden box, a cross between a coffin and an ammunition box. The view became more and more superb, a sea of mountain peaks and clouds, with nothing to left and right but sheer rock except an occasional lingering avalanche of snow. . . . We landed on a narrow ledge in the midst of a snow flurry, where the enemy may, if they wish, hurl shrapnel, and ascended a flight of high, narrow steps, some open, some covered, cut in the rock on the edge of the mountain. We ran up the open ones to avoid being peppered by the Cecchini, the Austrian sharpshooters. On a little saddle at the top stood a tiny, wooden shack, with two freshly killed fowl hanging from its eaves. The shack was the headquarters of Major Menotti Garibaldi, the commander of this post. . . .

Imagine the Italian side of this peak, held by Menotti for over a year: a mass of sheer whitish rock cut by steps, trenches, and paths, edged here and there by bags filled with sand or stones, honeycombed at different levels by tunnels and caverns, and hung with shacks sheltering men, food, and munitions, and, over it all, a great, shifting wind scattering a mixture of hail and snow, through which the sunlight momentarily breaks, changing entirely the aspect of the scene. Then imagine some six hundred staunch men blasting, drilling, cutting steps, placing poles and rails on every possible foothold of this peak, and other men sleeping, resting, or doing all sorts of jobs, from cooking to manning guns, in tunnels and caverns which are stacked with rifles and tin boxes containing gas masks, inscribed, "Chi lascia la Maschera MUORE"—he who throws away his gas mask dies. . . .

As we were inspecting a new path hewn out of the rock and leading to the uppermost line, a soldier approached, saluted, and said very quietly to Garibaldi, "So-and-so's hand has been blown off, blasting." Garibaldi asked briefly one or two questions to identify the man, then excused himself and left us, saying, "The good men always get it." Later we heard groans while passing the infirmary, a trim little shack built against the rock, where the stump of the man's arm was being dressed before he was sent down by *teleferica* to the foot of the mountain whither an ambulance had been summoned by telephone. This tragic conversion of a sturdy Alpino into a *mutilato*, who, on his transference to the normal world, must face the end of his career and real life, ran its course in quiet and orderly fashion. No anaesthetic was used in dressing his wound.

Noncombatant Voices from the War's Other Fronts

23

MARIE AND PAUL PIREAUD

Correspondence between a French Civilian and Her Husband in the Battle Zone

May 27, 1915, and May 23, 1916

As we have already seen in previous documents, many soldiers wrote home to their loved ones, and their letters were often treasured. In a few rare instances, both sides of a wartime correspondence have survived, as in the following letters exchanged by a young French couple, Marie and Paul Pireaud. Marie struggled to cope at home, noting in the spring of 1915 the difficulty of a task vital to a rural community, harvesting hay, when so many households lacked their male laborers. A year later, Paul tried to describe the unspeakable horrors of the Battle of Verdun, which were, in his words, "impossible" to convey.

My beloved Paul:
Now that Italy has mobilized do you believe that the war will be finished soon I saw in the paper yesterday that Greece Romania and Bulgaria are all going to get into the war during the summer if only this could bring us an end because as you know everything is bothering us we have lots of work. . . .

Anyway we are only doing what we can the most urgent. We are in the midst of haymaking that's going pretty well soon we will move over to the meadows at la Conterie.

The wheat is beautiful now with long stalks I don't really know but I think that lots of fodder crops and wheat are going to be lost imagine all the houses where there is only a woman and the children.

From Martha Hanna, ed. and trans., *Your Death Would Be Mine: Paul and Marie Pireaud in the Great War* (Cambridge, Mass.: Harvard University Press, 2006), 26, 78.

How sad the countryside is. When will we learn that these horrible things are finished Until then receive from your wife all her best kisses and her gentlest caresses love and kisses from the one who will love you forever

MARIE TO PAUL, 27 MAY 1915

* * *

Letter of an eyewitness: Verdun is impossible to describe. It is about 7 or 8 kilometers from here to Douaumont. Not a trench, not a communications trench, nothing but shell holes one inside another. There is not one piece of ground that is not turned up. To see what has been done here one could not imagine all the shells of all calibers that have been used. The holes made by the 300[-millimeter shells] could hold fifteen horses. There are no more woods. Shattered trees resemble telegraph poles. It is complete devastation. Not one square of land has been spared. One would have to come here to understand it. One cannot imagine such a thing.

Everything has been brought together on this part of the front. The cannon are mouth to mouth and never cease firing there is not one second when the cannon cease. There are no attacks right now but still there are losses. Shells fall and mow down everyone and everything without pity.

One can only go out at night to work this land that has been churned up a hundred times. The cadavers of swollen horses infect this immense battlefield. We make a trench, a shell lands, everything has to start over again if one is among the survivors. Attacks become impossible. When a troop wants to go out the artillery takes aim at it. There are too many guns everywhere. For as long as they are here both advance and retreat are impossible.

You can be sure that Verdun will not be taken. Here it is extermination on the ground without seeing the enemy. Soon we will be relieved. I wonder how I am still standing after all of this one is completely numb.

Men look at one another with wild eyes. It takes a real effort to hold a conversation.

PAUL PIREAUD, 23 MAY 1916

24

LESLIE A. DAVIS

Report on Armenian Genocide
June 30, 1915

While serving as U.S. consul in Harput, Turkey, from 1915 to 1917, Leslie Davis witnessed firsthand the Ottoman Empire's treatment of its Armenian inhabitants. He went into the countryside and saw bodies as well as other evidence that the "relocation" of the Armenian population was actually something far more pernicious. His report received little notice at the time but remains an important eyewitness record of this atrocity.

AMERICAN CONSULATE
MAMOURET-UL-AZIZ (HARPUT)
JUNE 30, 1915

Honorable Henry Morgenthau,
American Ambassador
Constantinople

Sir:

I have the honor to report to the Embassy about one of the severest measures ever taken by any government and one of the greatest tragedies in all history. If the Embassy had not already learned about it from other sources, my telegrams of June 27th and 28th and my brief dispatch of June 29th will have brought the matter to the attention of the Embassy. . . .

As stated in some of the above mentioned dispatches, a revolutionary movement on the part of some of the Armenians was discovered and severe measures were taken to check it. These were undertaken in a wholesale matter [*sic*], little distinction being made between people who were entirely innocent and those who were suspected of being participants in the movement. Practically every male Armenian of any

From Leslie A. Davis, *The Slaughterhouse Province: An American Diplomat's Report on the Armenian Genocide, 1914–1917*, ed. Susan K. Blair (New Rochelle, N.Y.: Aristide D. Caratzas, 1989), 143, 146–49.

consequence at all here has been arrested and put in prison. A great many of them were subjected to the most cruel tortures under which some of them died. Several hundred of the leading Armenians were sent away at night and it seems to be clearly established that most, if not all, of them were killed. Last week there were well founded rumors of a threatened massacre. I think there is very little doubt that one was planned.

Another method was found, however, to destroy the Armenian race. This is no less than the deportation of the entire Armenian population, not only from this Vilayet,[1] but, I understand, from all six Vilayets comprising Armenia. There are said to be about sixty thousand Armenians in this Vilayet and about a million in the six Vilayets. All of these are to be sent into exile; an undertaking greater, probably, than anything of the kind in all history. For several days last week there were rumors of this but it seemed incredible. . . .

It is impossible for me to give any adequate idea of the panic . . . that has resulted from the announcement of this order of expulsion. The people have been given four or six days to dispose of everything they have and leave. For the merchants to wind up their affairs in that short time is difficult. It is also difficult for householders to dispose of their household and personal effects. The result has been a panic such as has never been known here or in few other places. Every one who is obliged to leave is trying to get together a little money to take on the journey. The Turks are, of course, taking advantage of the situation to get things at practically nothing. Robbery and looting were never undertaken in a more wholesale manner. Turkish men and Turkish women are entering the houses of all the Armenians and taking things at almost any price. As nearly half the population are leaving they have to take what they can get. This is rarely more than five or ten per cent, of the value. All the furniture in a house, costing originally one or two hundred pounds will be sold for ten of fifteen pounds. Rugs that cost five or ten pounds are sold for fifty or seventy-five piasters. The people are glad to get anything at all for their merchandise or effects. The streets are full of camels carrying off the loot and of rich Turks and Turkish women dressed in their finest gowns, who are making a holiday of the occasion. The scene reminds one of a lot of hungry vultures hovering over the remains of those who have fallen by the way. A more disgusting sight than that which is taking place here now can scarcely be imagined. . . .

In my telegram of June 27th, I asked the Embassy to wire me also if it would be possible to secure exemption for the naturalized American

---

[1]The *vilayets* (the proper Turkish plural is *vilâyetler*) were the main administrative subdivisions of the Empire starting from the second half of the nineteenth century.

citizens who are here. I spoke to the Vali about this at once but he has been very evasive. I hope to receive some reply from the Embassy in time, if it [is] going to be possible to do anything to save any of these people and their children. There is one class of citizens who are certainly entitled to protection. There are women whose husbands are naturalized American citizens and are now in America, while they have returned here for a short time to visit relatives. There are several of these and nearly all of them have children with them who were born in America. I shall certainly do everything possible to save these.

Tomorrow the exodus of one-half of the population of this region commences. Were the people not so entirely subdued I should expect to see some stirring scenes. As it is, I can hardly think it possible that the authorities will succeed in sending everyone into exile, but as yet there does not seem to be any sign of their relenting or of their granting many exemptions.

I HAVE THE HONOR TO BE, SIR,
YOUR OBEDIENT SERVANT,
/SIGNED/
/LESLIE A. DAVIS,/
CONSUL.

25

VISCOUNT BRYCE REPORT ON ATROCITIES AGAINST ARMENIANS

Narrative of an Armenian Lady
November 2, 1915

As was the case with reports of atrocities committed by German troops in France and Belgium, the British government sought to document abuses conducted by the Ottoman Empire against its own population. A former professor of law and, in the decade before the war, the United Kingdom's ambassador to the United States, Viscount James Bryce (1838–1922)

From Viscount James Bryce, *The Treatment of Armenians in the Ottoman Empire, 1915–16: Documents Presented to Viscount Grey of Fallodon, Secretary of State for Foreign Affairs, by Viscount Bryce* (London: Sir Joseph Causton & Sons, 1916), 271–75.

was given responsibility for compiling evidence about abuses against civilians both in Belgium in 1915 and later in the Ottoman Empire. Both reports came under attack, especially after the war, for being propaganda riddled with lies. Yet when published in 1916, the official volume on massacres in the Ottoman Empire attempted to gather a wide range of evidence about abuses committed against Armenians. There were, of course, political motives to the gathering of evidence designed to discredit and condemn enemy nations. However, the evidence recorded here provides an important glimpse of what has long remained a forgotten and devastating act of total war: deliberate attacks on categories of persons—women, children, the elderly—meant to be protected during wartime. This first-person account by a female survivor could not be verified at the time, but its publication in an Armenian journal in New York in January 1916 contributed to the kinds of information publicly circulating about these attacks.

Shortly after last Easter (1915), the Turkish officials searched the Armenian churches and schools of G., H., C., AQ., AR., AS.[1] and the surrounding villages, but without finding anything incriminating. Afterwards they took the keys of these buildings, and filled them with soldiers. They also searched private houses on the pretence of looking for arms and ammunition, but they did not find anything. After that the Town Crier announced that all arms were to be handed over to the Government, and by this means a number of arms were collected. . . .

The Town Crier proclaimed that on the following Tuesday those from B. and C. Streets in the Town of H. would be deported, on Wednesday the Armenians from AQ., on Thursday those from AR., and so on.

CJ. and two hundred other Armenians were deported ten days before we were, that is on Wednesday, the 23rd June; we do not know their destination. Their party started at midnight. Some of them dropped cards asking for money, and at AT. money was conveyed to them. But the following Monday, the 28th June, when the Armenian women of AT. went to the river, they saw some Turkish women washing blood-stained clothes. The Armenian women took the clothes from the Turkish women and brought them to the Governor at G. The Governor on hearing this went to AT. and found that the Bishop [of H.] and the 200 Armenians had been killed. . . .

---

[1]Throughout this document, the names of people and places were obscured with a simple encryption to maintain confidentiality.

All the people of C. started the same day. I think we were about 600 families. We had with us all our cattle and all our property. The first night we reached AU. and slept that night in the fields. The next day we passed many corpses heaped together under bridges and on the road; their blood had collected in pools. Probably these were the Armenians that were killed with the Bishop, for the corpses were all those of men. We spent the night near AV. in a valley, and that night we had to drink water polluted with blood. We promised our guards money if they took us [to] a better road and gave us clean water. The third day they again made us travel past corpses, and on Wednesday we reached A. . . .

We were already within a short distance of Diyarbekir when two soldiers came from the Governor, to find out where we had been during the last nine days. Here the gendarmes that were with us took away all our cows and cattle; they also kidnapped one woman and two girls. Outside the walls of Diyarbekir, we had to sit in the burning sun for 24 hours. That same day a number of Turks came from the city and kidnapped our little girls. Towards evening again we went on, still crying; more Turks came to carry off our girls and young brides, and would not let us even open our mouths to protest. Then we left all our cattle and everything we had, to save our honour and our lives. It was already night when the Turks from Diyarbekir attacked us three times and carried off the girls and young brides who had fallen behind. After this we lost all sense of time. The next morning again the gendarmes searched us all over, and then made us march six hours. During these six hours we found no drinking water, and many women sank on the way from thirst and hunger. The third day after that they robbed us, and violated us near a place where there was water. Some days after, two Turks dressed in white coats followed us, and, every time they had a chance, carried off still more of our girls. The wife of CS. Effendi from C. had three daughters, one of whom was married. A coloured gendarme who was with us wanted to take these girls. The mother resisted, and was thrown over a bridge by one of the Turks. The poor woman broke her arm, but her mule-driver dragged her up again. Again the same Turks threw her down, with one of her daughters, from the top of the mountain. The moment the married daughter saw her mother and sister thrown down, she thrust the baby in her arms upon another woman, ran after them crying "Mother, mother!" and threw herself down the same precipice. Some said that one of the Turkish officers went down after them and finished them off. After that Mrs. CS.'s remaining daughter and I disguised ourselves, and, each taking a child in our arms, abandoned everything and walked to Mardin. There our party joined us again. We stayed there eight days. There was an artificial lake there, and every night they opened the sluices and flooded the ground, so that in the panic they might kidnap some of the girls. They also attacked us every night and kidnapped little children. At last, one evening, they drove us on again and left us among the mountains. They wounded a woman because she did not wish to give up her daughter. When they were going to carry off another girl, I asked CT. Tchaoush, a Mardin man, to help us. He stopped them at once, and did not let them take her away.

26

LENA GUILBERT FORD

Keep the Home Fires Burning

1915

While the audience for poetic and literary evocations of the war might have been limited to the literate populations who could read, songs accompanied armies on the march and soothed those waiting at home. Here is perhaps the war's most famous song in English. It was a popular hit, with music by the British actor Ivor Novello (1893–1951) and words by Lena Guilbert Ford (1870–1918), an American living in London who was killed along with her son in an air raid in March 1918. Its sentimentality is unabashed, and it calls on those at home to do their part for the war effort by keeping the hearth fires of domestic life alive despite fears and anxiety.

> They were summoned from the hillside;
> They were called in from the glen.
> And the Country found them ready
> At the stirring call for men.
> Let no tears add to their hardship,
> As the Soldiers pass along
> And although your heart is breaking
> Make it sing this cheery song.

Lena Guilbert Ford, "Keep the Home Fires Burning," music by Ivor Novello (London: Ascherberg, Hopwood & Crew, 1915).

Refrain:
Keep the Home-fires burning,
While your hearts are yearning
Though your lads are far away
They dream of Home;
There's a silver lining
Through the dark cloud shining,
Turn the dark cloud inside out,
Till the boys come Home.

Over seas there came a pleading
["]Help a Nation in distress"
And we gave our glorious laddies;
Honour bade us do no less.
For no gallant Son of freedom
To a tyrant[']s yoke should bend,
And a noble heart must answer
To the sacred call of "Friend[.]"

Refrain:
Keep the Home-fires burning,
While your hearts are yearning
Though your lads are far away
They dream of Home;
There's a silver lining
Through the dark cloud shining,
Turn the dark cloud inside out,
Till the boys come Home[.]

27

Berlin Police Reports

February 17 and October 17, 1915

As early as 1915, the German government imposed the rationing of basic foodstuffs, and such rationing only tightened as the war continued. In these two accounts from 1915, women in Berlin respond to the growing food shortages resulting from the Allied blockade of Germany. The German government was not the only one to record the grievances of its civilian population. However, concern over the potentially destabilizing actions of these mainly female crowds led to an intense focus on their behavior, as seen in these police accounts written within a few days of the protests they describe. The women felt that their contributions to the war effort went unappreciated, and such protests grew in intensity and violence as the war—and the lack of food and necessities—continued.

FEBRUARY 17, 1915

On the 16th of the month at 5:00 p.m., thousands of women and children gathered at the municipal market hall in Andreas Street to buy a few pounds of potatoes. As the sale commenced, everyone stormed the market stands. The police, who were trying to keep order, were simply overrun and were powerless against the onslaught. A life-threatening press at the stands ensued; each sought to get past the next. . . . [W]omen had their possessions ripped from them and children were trampled on the ground as they pleaded for help. . . . [W]omen who got away from the crowds with some ten pounds of potatoes each were bathed in sweat and dropped to their knees from exhaustion before they could continue home.

—REPORT OF OFFICER RHEIN

✶ ✶ ✶

OCTOBER 17, 1915

After 25 minutes I entered Edison St. in Öberschoneweide [just outside Berlin] and then turning onto Wilhelm St. came upon a crowd of several

---

"Berlin Police Reports." Belinda Davis, trans., in *Lives and Voices: Sources in European Women's History*, ed. Lisa Di Caprio and Merry E. Wiesner (Belmont, Calif.: Wadsworth Publishing, 2000), 426–27.

thousand men and women, who were loudly howling and pushing the policemen aside. I learned from the sergeant on duty, who had received several head injuries . . . that the crowd had already stormed several butter shops because of the prices. . . . [S]everal large display windows were shattered, shop doors destroyed, and entire stocks were simply taken. . . . I was asked to close off the street as the police and officers were completely helpless against the crowd. We cleared the street with fifteen mounted officers. . . . Various objects such as flower pots were thrown at us.
— REPORT OF OFFICER KRUPPHAUSEN

28

Resolutions Adopted by the International Congress of Women at The Hague

May 1, 1915

Protesting over food shortages was not the only way in which women reacted to the war. During the war's first year, women from across most of the belligerent and neutral states — mainly activists who had previously been campaigning for women's suffrage — came together at a peace congress in The Hague. Claiming a unique perspective as women, as members of their states who nonetheless lacked voting rights and thus any decision-making power with regard to war, and as those who claimed to feel the war's enormous costs, they passed a series of resolutions. In the aftermath of the congress, a newly formed organization, the Women's International League (later "for Peace and Freedom"), and its leadership, including future Nobel Peace Prize winner (1931) Jane Addams, spoke to various heads of government in an effort to urge an immediate, negotiated settlement of the war. Though willing to meet with the league's representatives, government leaders were not ready to seek a negotiated peace. Here are some of the resolutions passed by the congress, reflective of those who called for peace in the midst of war.

From "Appendix 3: Resolutions Adopted by the International Congress of Women at The Hague, May 1, 1915," in Jane Addams, Emily G. Balch, and Alice Hamilton, *Women at The Hague: The International Congress of Women and Its Results* (New York: Macmillan, 1915), 150–52.

Women and War

PROTEST

We women, in International Congress assembled, protest against the madness and the horror of war, involving as it does a reckless sacrifice of human life and the destruction of so much that humanity has laboured through centuries to build up.

WOMEN'S SUFFERING IN WAR

This International Congress of Women opposes the assumption that women can be protected under the conditions of modern warfare. It protests vehemently against the odious wrongs of which women are the victims in time of war, and especially against the horrible violation of women which attends all war.

Action towards Peace

THE PEACE SETTLEMENT

This International Congress of Women of different nations, classes, creeds and parties is united in expressing sympathy with the suffering of all, whatever their nationality, who are fighting for their country or labouring under the burden of war.

Since the mass of the people in each of the countries now at war believe themselves to be fighting, not as aggressor but in self-defence and for their national existence, there can be no irreconcilable differences between them, and their common ideals afford a basis upon which a magnanimous and honourable peace might be established. The Congress therefore urges the Governments of the world to put an end to this bloodshed, and to begin peace negotiations. It demands that the peace which follows shall be permanent and therefore based on principles of justice, including those laid down in the resolutions adopted by this Congress, namely:

That no territory should be transferred without the consent of the men and women in it, and that the right of conquest should not be recognized.

That autonomy and a democratic parliament should not be refused to any people.

That the Governments of all nations should come to an agreement to refer future international disputes to arbitration or conciliation and to bring social, moral and economic pressure to bear upon any country which resorts to arms.

That foreign politics should be subject to democratic control.
That women should be granted equal political rights with men.

29

MARIA DOBLER BENEMANN

Visé (After a Letter from the Field)
1915

Those deemed apart from the war and its brutality, notably women at home, nonetheless learned of wartime horrors from the men at arms in their lives. The German writer Maria Dobler Benemann (1887–1979) was living with her two children while her husband fought on the western front. He died in 1914, and she used both his letters to her and the stories told to her by those home on leave to translate the occupation of a Belgian town into a poetic evocation of war and its costs for all civilians. The poem appeared in print in 1915. Benemann spent the remainder of the war writing, aiding victims of the war, and ultimately taking a public stand against the war toward its end.

Smoke-black the air, the city in rubble,
buildings reduced to beams all charred
that strew the streets like barricades.
No roof shields the weary, just distant stars.

On paving stones troops take hard rest,
barely covered by a coat.
Around, fatigue-dulled men breathe deep,
while you alone lie awake so late.

Behind, a heap of ashes haunts you,
an elegant house that you transformed
when hunting for a sniper's nest.

Maria Dobler Benemann, "Visé (After a Letter from the Field)," in *Lines of Fire: Women Writers of World War I*, ed. Margaret R. Higonnet (New York: Plume, 1999), 484–85.

One room still held an instrument,
above it a fearful Virgin hung:
the quiet greeting and silent respite
caught you in their sudden embrace.

As light waned you plucked some chords,
hollow echoes of the home's dead souls.
The Queen you salvaged in your coat
to bring her to me, when you make peace.

Then set fresh flames: you do your duty,
blow this house up like all the rest.
. . . Was that a cry? or just a broken string?
Music, music behind you has collapsed.

30

EDITHA VON KRELL

Recollections of Four Months Working in a German Munitions Factory

1917

Since the time that factories and mills came into being, women had worked in them, and in this sense women's wartime industrial work was nothing new. However, certain aspects of women's work during the First World War indicated that something innovative was indeed happening. For one thing, even women who had been accustomed to factory work found new types of occupations open to them for the first time. For another, while their wages were never equal to those of men, women could earn a good deal more money working for the war effort than many had in prewar years. Munitions work, particularly, was seen as a patriotic duty, as this account by Editha von Krell shows. Krell, a privileged and educated woman, also discovered a solidarity that could be

From "*Deutsche Frauen, Deutsche Treue*" (German Women, German and Loyal) in *The Virago Book of Women and the Great War*, ed. Joyce Marlow (London: Virago, 1998), 255–57.

found among all women by undertaking work that was at once tedious and risky—making weapons meant dealing with volatile chemicals, and some munitions workers died or became ill from their work—and yet ultimately fulfilling. For Krell, the sheer physical strain of the labor was surprising and exhausting, but as she recalls, her working-class coworkers helped her out when it became too much for her. Although her four months in the factory gave her insight into how other German women lived, since her motivation was patriotism rather than necessity, there were limits to the sympathy that she and others like her would have for munitions workers who later went on strike to protest their wages and working conditions, and eventually the war itself.

As the war went on, the "WUMBA" (Berlin Weapons and Munitions Production Office for Field Artillery) ordered two large munitions factories to be built right next to our town too. But very soon there was a shortage of male workers there. And so, at the end of April 1917, all the town's women and girls were asked to come and work in these factories. At the time this seemed to be the most important assistance one could offer, and when we heard from the captain running the factories that no one from the educated classes had yet volunteered, and that hundreds of workers were urgently required, our decision was made. Together with two friends, my sister and I volunteered for duty immediately.

All we had to do was make the necessary purchases: large long-sleeved aprons; an enamel dish and spoon for our evening meal; a coffee pot and mug and a light straw bag in which all these items could be properly stowed away, together with our bread and margarine. Then, somewhat apprehensively, given the completely unknown situation that lay before us, we set off for the factory for the first time.

We began with an eight-hour shift from 3 in the afternoon until 11 in the evening. We were supposed to have changed shifts the following week, but we agreed with our work-mates that we would always work the "night shift."

Every day we left our parental home at just after 2 p.m. A twenty-minute walk took us to a small temporary station, where we boarded a worker's train for a fifteen-minute ride which took us close to the factory; then we had another five-minute walk to the work-sheds of the Bürgerfelde Munitions Factory.

Initially we were all put in the sewing room, where day after day we had to sew thousands of little bags which were then filled with barrel powder for the cartridges in another department. We felt as if we had been transported back to our school days—except that our school benches had been far more comfortable than the rough wooden benches without back rests on which we had to sit here. We sewed without interruption—apart from a short coffee break and a half-hour supper break, when we could straighten ourselves up again and stretch our legs. Supervisors walked up and down, inspecting our sewing and making sure that the conversation amongst the more than 100 female workers gathered in the room didn't grow too loud. Our backs often hurt from this unaccustomed sitting. Our heads often ached terribly in the bad air, which you could almost have cut with a knife. But we carried out this uninteresting work very conscientiously. We scored a psychological success too. Following our example, around 70 young girls volunteered for duty.

After a few days my sister was posted to the office, which was in urgent need of assistance. She had passed her Abitur[1] and teaching exams, so she was best suited to fill this post. She was responsible for working out the quantities of powder, cartridge cases and fuses needed for the ammunition trains commissioned, and for ensuring that any materials the factory was short of were ordered in good time—

After a few weeks, at our own request, we were moved on to "heavy work," where we had to put the howitzer shells together with the brass cases containing the powder, and equip them with fuses.—It was hard work and required a good deal of energy; all the more so because the air in the relatively low barrack was often unbearable. For despite the heat—it was July by now—we were not allowed to air the rooms, even during our meal breaks. Doors and windows had to be kept permanently shut because of the danger of explosions. But we prided ourselves on never slacking, on always keeping up with the professional workers. Here too the harmonious relationships we enjoyed with them was clear. For if ever this completely unaccustomed work proved too much for one of us, one of the workers would help out as a matter of course, smiling, "Leave that to me, miss—it's far too hard for you!" We never really thought about the immediate danger we were in. But during this time three young girls, who had recently started work in the other munitions factory, were fatally injured by a grenade which fell and exploded.

Even today we still like to think back to the time when we were able to serve the Fatherland, working with our hands at one with the people.

---

[1] Abitur is the exam taken when leaving secondary school in Germany.

31

PHILIPPE VERNEUIL

Le Départ

1917

Once the orders for mobilization came in 1914, troops across the continent set forth. As the war progressed, each year new classes of military conscripts joined the conflict. By 1916, even Britain had retreated from having a solely volunteer army. During the first months of the conflict, there was no respite for troops, and the fighting remained brisk. After it became clear that the war was going to last far longer than anticipated, governments began to permit their soldiers leaves to return home or at least to sojourn beyond the battlefield. Train stations in the major European capitals thus became scenes for emotional homecomings and leave-takings. Here, Philippe Verneuil (the pseudonym of Philippe Soupault [1897–1990], a French poet, writer, and activist associated after the war with surrealism) tries to capture the mood of farewell in starkly modern verse.

The hour
for Farewell

The crowd turns around
an agitated man
The cries
of women around me
Each one rushes forward
jostling me.
Here
when the evening falls,
I'm cold.

From Philippe Verneuil (alias Philippe Soupault), "Départ," in *Les Poètes de la Grande Guerre*, ed. Jacques Béal (Paris: le Cherche Midi, 1992), 20. Translated by Susan R. Grayzel, 2010.

32

RAINER MARIA RILKE

Letter to Joachim von Winterfeldt-Menkin on the Death of His Soldier Friend

September 16, 1918

Many citizens of warring states far from combat zones wrote to one another to offer their perspectives on the war and, in far too many cases, to provide condolences for wartime losses, as in this letter by one of the most acclaimed German-language poets of the time, Rainer Maria Rilke (1875–1926). Born in Prague and the holder of an Austro-Hungarian passport, Rilke was educated in Munich and Berlin and spent time in Russia and France before the war broke out. Initially enthusiastic about the war's arrival, he soon became disillusioned. In 1915, at forty years of age, he was drafted into the Austrian army. He spent a brief time serving at the military archives in Vienna but never saw combat. Toward the end of the war, Rilke wrote this letter to Joachim von Winterfeldt-Menkin after the death of their friend Bernard von der Marwitz in a field hospital near Valenciennes, France. In it, Rilke reflects on what the loss of this promising young man—and perhaps, by extension, a generation of young men—might mean for the future of Germany.

Again and again since your letter came, my dear Herr von Winterfeldt, I have taken up my pen and tried and have no command of the words the moment calls for. Which are they? Have we not long since given out all those adapted to the various demands of grief? Anything there might still be to say we would have to break off with a piece of our heart—, it lies beyond exaggeration, beyond any extreme ever possible to words, and the excess of mourning for the dead that threatens to break out presupposes, in order still to be kept within bounds at all, an infinite extension of soul in us which again cannot have developed in such a tangled and chaotic time.

What shall I say: I know, I feel, you have lost a young friend, the best, the biggest, the incomparable thing that in essence these two words can

From Rainer Maria Rilke, *Wartime Letters of Rainer Maria Rilke, 1914–1921*, trans. M. D. Herter Norton (New York: W. W. Norton, 1968), 91–93.

stand for. Among the thousands of young men who have sacrificed their own, specially intended lives in the impenetrable destiny of the war, Bernard von der Marwitz will remain, to those who knew him, one of the most unforgotten. The memorial you are gathering for him in your heart will have more than personal significance. For the "being young" and the "being friend" of this young man of fine culture and large capacity for emotion was a more than personal manifestation, was in a certain sense standard for that German youth which, without the interruption of such fearful disturbances, would have assured our future in a wide-open spiritual world. The continued and inextricable wrong of the war has called up more and more young people of contradictory mind, who think to deduce the future more cleanly out of the negation of the past. In Marwitz, on the contrary, tradition functioned together with a perfect readiness for intellectually responsible freedom: if a future is to come out of German youth, it must be an attitude very closely related to his that would be determinative for it. So the thought of his survival, it seems to me, is linked with those most intimate hopes that we have yet to direct towards life which is altogether to be rescued.

I cannot at the moment, dear Herr von Winterfeldt, do more to comfort you than admit with entire conviction the great and unique worth of your friend.

33

ETHEL BILBROUGH

Diary Entry Describing a Zeppelin Raid in England

October 13, 1915

As a modern total war, the First World War presented civilians with conditions starkly different from those in many previous wars. In this diary entry, Mrs. Ethel Bilbrough describes the experience of her first zeppelin raid in October 1915. Airpower made civilians such as Bilbrough, who lived in Chislehurst, Kent, subject to bombing raids in places far removed from the so-called front lines. Although privileged, Bilbrough was not

From Private Papers of E. M. Bilbrough, 90/10/1, Department of Documents, Imperial War Museum, London.

immune from the new dangers that all civilians potentially faced in this war. She not only recorded her reactions but also took note of the extent to which zeppelin attacks killed and injured people and destroyed parts of London, even going so far as to include news clippings in her journal.

(We experience our *first raid!*)
WEDNESDAY 13TH OCT. 1915

Being the night of our harvest festival, A. and I went to church, as, war or no war, there's no reason why people shouldn't be grateful for a splendid harvest.

It was a lovely night—not a cloud to be seen; a fine night for Zepplins, and an ideal one for a raid! So it proved; for on coming out of church after a nice peaceful service about "ploughing fields" and "harvest homes," we found Chislehurst in a most unusual state of commotion! Excited groups hung about the church porch, & we caught fragmentary bits of conversation about "bombs,["] and "shells," and "guns"!

In spite of the myriads of stars it was very dark there being no moon,—goodness knows where it had got to, (scared away I should think by the attrocities of mankind!) [.] Coming home one found it expedient to walk in the middle of the road, which seemed the only place where one couldn't break one's ankle over the unseen curb, or barge into a gate or a lamp-post!—none of which are lit now owing to the new lighting regulations. Coming along Willow Grove we met a man (in a state of abject terror,) who stopped us and asked if we had "*seen the Zepplins*"? He was an extremely poor and common man; but excitement & danger makes everyone equal!

Things seem'd to quiet down after that, and as we walked down Walden Road and came out at the opening at the end, there was nothing to be seen but a great arc of indigo blue sky scintillating with countless stars. A few stragglers hung about the lodges as if half hoping to hear another gun! but it was all as silent as the grave, and we slipped quietly into the grange as the servants were all abed (that sounds nice & old fashioned!) and retired for the night. But somehow I couldn't sleep to save my life, everything was so quiet, but I heard imaginary noises & held my breath listening. So an hour or two passed, and then quite audibly & *quite* unmistakably a canon went off, bang-bang, bang, bang, *bang*!! and (extremely alarmed,) I woke up Ken—sleeping the sleep of the just! A Zepplin raid either makes a person intensely valiant, or a pitiful coward!!

Ken was annoyed at being disturbed, and muttering something about "Gott strafen the Kaiser," ["God punish the Kaiser"] turned over & went to sleep again! But the great guns at Woolwich (only six miles away) went on thundering away, and I wondered what was going on, and whether destruction and suffering & loss of life were really & truly taking place so near at hand. Things in the paper always seem so far away, it's only when one sees and hears *for oneself,* that the real horrors of war becomes apparent. Then presently amid the booming of guns, came a terrific sort of explosion, like a crash of several canon going off altogether, and whatever it was, I knew it was something deathly,—probably a bomb, and out of bed I hopped & lit a candle. The air seemed alive with horrid weird uncanny sounds, and there is something terrifying in the thought that two miles up above one in space there is a merciless enemy dropping incendiary bombs promiscuously on whatever comes handy!!

Ken actually *did* get up then (of his own free will!) & got into a dressing gown, & we went into the oriel room in the dark.

There the window was all alight with the reflection of searchlights, and shells from our guns being hurled up into the sky trying to reach the Zepplin, and then as we got to the window, a shell burst just like a firework, with a lurid red light. But we *never* reach the Zepplins, which (*two miles* high) merely look down on our breaking shells fathoms below, & laugh! It was horribly cold standing there shivering in the dark room & watching weird things going on in the heavens, and Ken soon observed that he was "going back to bed." As there seem'd nothing else to be done I followed suit, but sleep didn't come for the rest of the night, and I was very thankful to see the early dawn steal through the curtains and know that this nightmare of a night was ended. But the Zepplins wrought havoc, and *forty two* people failed to escape, eight were killed, and the others seriously hurt. Bombs were dropped on Woolwich where much damage was done (that was the strange uncanny sound I heard) and almost 40 fell on Croydon, while London was fiercely attacked. One side of the Strand was completely wrecked, and Ken said he went and saw where one bomb had fallen in the street, and there was a hole in the solid Concrete, four ft deep!—it had gone through like a red hot needle in a piece of butter! No wonder people are afraid of such demoniacal inventions; they would go slick through a house and anything (or anyone) who came in their way! All the trains were held up so that their light should be no guide, and the 8 o'clock train from town never got to Elmstead [train station] till 1 o'clock! I heard it come in, but little thought what train it was! It (the train) made an impression on me, for after the strain & anxiety of listening to unknown & terrifying sounds,—sounds *never* heard before,—, the puffing & snorting of a railway train sounded friendly & sympathetic, & gave one a feeling of security & relief!

Next day the papers made light of it all, saying only 8 were killed and 30 wounded, but that was only up to 11.30. I *felt* that there would be fresh revelations after 12 o'clock. Later on it was announced there were no fewer that 170 casualties, & over 40 deaths which is awful;—five were children. Many parts of London were wrecked, including part of the Lyceum theatre, where some people were killed, and part of the Strand is in a state of complete ruin. Bombs were simply rained down on Croydon where eight people were killed in one house, and at Woolwich (near here) great damage was done, and bombs went clean through two churches there. So that was what we heard; not merely the firing of our canon *at* the Zepplins, but their own dastardly murderous bombs falling & exploding on our innocent civilians within a few miles of us.

34

MARIA DEGRUTÈRE

Diary Entries from a Civilian in Occupied France

March 1915–April 1916

Civilians living under occupation faced particular difficulties. In this excerpt from the journal of Maria Degrutère, a Catholic school teacher living with her family in northern France, some of the common and frightening aspects of civilians living in territories occupied by foreign armies emerge. Since such armies could commandeer supplies at will, the cost and scarcity of food and fuel continually alarmed the local population, who did their best to surmount these difficulties. Civilians also shared the risk of damage and loss of life from bombardments, adding another element of danger to already fraught circumstances. Additionally,

From Maria Degrutère, "Tableau des événements particuliers et journaliers," in *Journaux de Combattants & Civils dans la France du Nord dans La Grande Guerre*, ed. Annette Becker (Villeneuve-d'Ascq, France: Presses Universitaires du Septentrion, 1998), 176–78, 191, 193, 195, 197. Translated by Susan R. Grayzel, 2010.

by the midpoint of the war, the occupying German army began to requisition the labor that the French and other captive populations could supply. One of the most infamous of such "forced labor" campaigns came during Easter week 1916, when young people and especially girls were forcibly removed from their homes in places such as Lille. As Degrutère explains here, the reactions of their families were "heartbreaking."

1915

March 27 The Germans are making all the old people from hospitals and 1,000 women and children leave Roubaix, Tourcoing, and Mouvaux destined for France via Switzerland. This has caused general desolation, but it seems that the French government does not want it.

April 1-2-3 Another round of violent cannon and artillery fire.

April 4 A sad Easter. One finds white bread at the bakers, but for 3 francs for two pounds.

April 16-17-18-19 They are firing at planes daily. At the Madeleine, fragments of shells and shrapnel fall in many streets but happily without hurting anyone.

May 1-2 Violent artillery fire.

May 3 Many planes visit us. One French one, among others, came under cannon fire. Unhappily, a bomb fell near the central market and in exploding killed 3 people and wounded 9 others.

May 4-5 Always violent aerial combat. One must take shelter because of the splinters from shells. One even finds a piece on the sidewalk.

May 9 At 3:45 in the morning awakened with a start by the noise of 2 bombs dropped by a French plane: one on the Kommandantur . . . , the other on the Madeleine train station. A tremendous explosion, all the houses shook, including ours.

1916

January 1, midnight [G]unshots no longer make us afraid, we are used to them, but when one hears a terrible cannon roar, the window of our room dances a polka, it's truly grim.

January 16   The English bomb Lille from 10 in the evening until 4 in the morning. Shells fell on the summer palace—Boulevard de la Liberté—quai de Waulz—on the citadel—the St. Sauveur train station. Inhabitants of Lille are panic-stricken.

We now have a very sad life, we are at the mercy of bombardments, explosions, contagious diseases.

January 28   Terrible cannon fire all day.

March   Life has now become unbearable. One can no longer find butter, eggs, milk, meat, or potatoes. We have bread, but it is of very bad quality, the shops are empty. Horse meat costs 10* per pound—an old cheese 8*. No more vegetables, shoes, fabric. . . . The Germans, having already taken the cows, sheep, pigs, and chickens, are now demanding the rabbits.

April 23   A sad Easter. Necessities of life have become more and more rare, we had only bread and rice for dinner not having anything else. The weather played a part, it rained without stopping, the water rose higher and higher in the cellars. . . . [Finally, the Germans are forcing families to leave.] Life becomes more and more painful on all sides. This carrying off of people lasted all week in Lille. Each day German soldiers (20 per house) with bayonets arrive in a neighborhood around 3 in the morning, waking everyone and carrying off some men, but above all women and young girls from 20 to 35 years of age to take them who knows where. There are indescribable scenes, hours of anguish and agony for mothers who have had their children wrested from them. Many people faint, others go mad, some are crazy enough to try to fight with the officers. Many of our friends have had to endure this terrible ordeal. . . . It's a heartbreaking spectacle.

35

V. I. LENIN

April Theses

April 7, 1917

Russia's war effort collapsed in a wave of strikes and mutinies early in 1917, which quickly led to a full-scale revolution that toppled the Romanov dynasty. In the aftermath, Vladimir Ilyich Lenin, the exiled Marxist revolutionary leader, returned to Russia in April 1917 and published what became known as the "April Theses" in Pravda. *As leader of the Bolsheviks, he offered his views on Russia's need to leave the war and how to prepare for a markedly different future.*

Introduction

I did not arrive in Petrograd until the night of April 3, and therefore at the meeting on April 4, I could, of course, deliver the report on the tasks of the revolutionary proletariat only on my own behalf, and with reservations as to insufficient preparation.

The only thing I could do to make things easier for myself—and for *honest* opponents—was to prepare the theses *in writing*. I read them out, and gave the text to Comrade Tsereteli. I read them *twice* very slowly: first at a meeting of Bolsheviks and then at a meeting of both Bolsheviks and Mensheviks.

I publish these personal theses of mine with only the briefest explanatory notes, which were developed in far greater detail in the report.

Theses

1. In our attitude towards the war, which under the new [provisional] government of [Georgy] Lvov and Co. unquestionably remains on Russia's part a predatory imperialist war owing to the capitalist nature of that

From V. I. Lenin, "The Tasks of the Proletariat in the Present Revolution, (a.k.a. April Theses)," trans. Isaacs Bernard, 2005, Marxists Internet Archive, www.marxists.org/archive/lenin/works/1917/apr/04.htm.

government, not the slightest concession to "revolutionary defencism"[1] is permissible.

The class-conscious proletariat can give its consent to a revolutionary war, which would really justify revolutionary defencism, only on condition: (a) that the power pass to the proletariat and the poorest sections of the peasants aligned with the proletariat; (b) that all annexations be renounced in deed and not in word; (c) that a complete break be effected in actual fact with all capitalist interests.

In view of the undoubted honesty of those broad sections of the mass believers in revolutionary defencism who accept the war only as a necessity, and not as a means of conquest, in view of the fact that they are being deceived by the bourgeoisie, it is necessary with particular thoroughness, persistence and patience to explain their error to them, to explain the inseparable connection existing between capital and the imperialist war, and to prove that without overthrowing capital *it is impossible* to end the war by a truly democratic peace, a peace not imposed by violence.

The most widespread campaign for this view must be organised in the army at the front.

Fraternisation.

2. The specific feature of the present situation in Russia is that the country is *passing* from the first stage of the revolution—which, owing to the insufficient class-consciousness and organisation of the proletariat, placed power in the hands of the bourgeoisie—to its *second stage*, which must place power in the hands of the proletariat and the poorest sections of the peasants.

This transition is characterised, on the one hand, by a maximum of legally recognised rights (Russia is *now* the freest of all the belligerent countries in the world); on the other, by the absence of violence towards the masses, and, finally, by their unreasoning trust in the government of capitalists, those worst enemies of peace and socialism.

This peculiar situation demands of us an ability to adapt ourselves to the *special* conditions of Party work among unprecedentedly large masses of proletarians who have just awakened to political life.

3. No support for the Provisional Government; the utter falsity of all its promises should be made clear, particularly of those relating to the renunciation of annexations. Exposure in place of the impermissible,

---

[1] Practice after the February Revolution and supported by moderate Socialists to urge military forces to continue the war "to defend the Revolution" while a peace negotiation was worked out, a policy that Lenin and the Bolsheviks opposed.

illusion-breeding "demand" that *this* government, a government of capitalists, should *cease* to be an imperialist government.

4. Recognition of the fact that in most of the Soviets of Workers' Deputies[2] our Party is in a minority, so far a small minority, as against a *bloc of all* the petty-bourgeois opportunist elements, from the Popular Socialists and the Socialist-Revolutionaries down to the Organising Committee (Chkheidze, Tsereteli, etc.), Steklov, etc., etc., who have yielded to the influence of the bourgeoisie and spread that influence among the proletariat.

The masses must be made to see that the Soviets of Workers' Deputies are the *only possible* form of revolutionary government, and that therefore our task is, as long as *this* government yields to the influence of the bourgeoisie, to present a patient, systematic, and persistent explanation of the errors of their tactics, an *explanation* especially adapted to the practical needs of the masses.

As long as we are in the minority we carry on the work of criticising and exposing errors and at the same time we preach the necessity of transferring the entire state power to the Soviets of Workers' Deputies, so that the people may overcome their mistakes by experience.

5. Not a parliamentary republic—to return to a parliamentary republic from the Soviets of Workers' Deputies would be a retrograde step—but a republic of Soviets of Workers', Agricultural Labourers' and Peasants' Deputies throughout the country, from top to bottom.

Abolition of the police, the army and the bureaucracy.

The salaries of all officials, all of whom are elective and displaceable at any time, not to exceed the average wage of a competent worker.

6. The weight of emphasis in the agrarian programme to be shifted to the Soviets of Agricultural Labourers' Deputies.

Confiscation of all landed estates. . . .

7. The immediate union of all banks in the country into a single bank, and the institution of control over it by the Soviet of Workers' Deputies.

8. It is not our *immediate* task to "introduce" socialism, but only to bring social production and the distribution of products at once under the *control* of the Soviets of Workers' Deputies.

---

[2] *Soviet* in Russian means council or committee; many such Soviets sprung up throughout Russia during the 1917 revolution. The largest Soviet in Petrograd represented one of the two entities struggling for power and attempting to share power during the phase of the Russian Revolution that followed the collapse of the Romanov dynasty. The other institution vying for power was the Provisional Government; the views of the Soviet were more radical. Lenin and the Bolsheviks would eventually use the Soviet as their base of support when they launched the October Revolution.

9. Party tasks:

(a) Immediate convocation of a Party congress;

(b) Alteration of the Party Programme, mainly:

(1) On the question of imperialism and the imperialist war,

(2) On our attitude towards the state and *our* demand for a "commune state";

(3) Amendment of our out-of-date minimum programme;

(c) Change of the Party's name.

10. A new International.

We must take the initiative in creating a revolutionary International, an International against the *social-chauvinists* and against the "Centre."

In order that the reader may understand why I had especially to emphasise as a rare exception the "case" of honest opponents, I invite him to compare the above theses with the following objection by Mr. Goldenberg: Lenin, he said, "has planted the banner of civil war in the midst of revolutionary democracy" (quoted in No. 5 of Mr. Plekhanov's *Yedinstvo*).

Isn't it a gem?

I write, announce and elaborately explain: "In view of the undoubted honesty of those *broad* sections of the *mass* believers in revolutionary defencism . . . in view of the fact that they are being deceived by the bourgeoisie, it is necessary with *particular* thoroughness, persistence and *patience* to explain their error to them. . . ."

Yet the bourgeois gentlemen who call themselves Social-Democrats, who *do not* belong either to the *broad* sections or to the *mass* believers in defencism, with serene brow present my view thus: "The banner[!] of civil war" (of which there is not a word in the theses and not a word in my speech!) has been planted(!) "in the midst[!!] of revolutionary democracy. . . ."

What does this mean? In what way does this differ from riot-inciting agitation, from *Russkaya Volya*[3]?

I write, announce and elaborately explain: "The Soviets of Workers' Deputies are the *only possible* form of revolutionary government, and therefore our task is to present a patient, systematic, and persistent *explanation* of the errors of their tactics, an explanation especially adapted to the practical needs of the masses."

[3]A middle-class newspaper published during the war in Petrograd.

Yet opponents of a certain brand present my views as a call to "civil war in the midst of revolutionary democracy"!

I attacked the Provisional Government for *not* having appointed an early date or any date at all, for the convocation of the Constituent Assembly, and for confining itself to promises. I argued that *without* the Soviets of Workers' and Soldiers' Deputies the convocation of the Constituent Assembly is not guaranteed and its success is impossible.

And the view is attributed to me that I am opposed to the speedy convocation of the Constituent Assembly!

I would call this "raving," had not decades of political struggle taught me to regard honesty in opponents as a rare exception.

Mr. Plekhanov in his paper called my speech "raving." Very good, Mr. Plekhanov! But look how awkward, uncouth and slow-witted you are in your polemics. If I delivered a raving speech for two hours, how is it that an audience of hundreds tolerated this "raving"? Further, why does your paper devote a whole column to an account of the "raving"? Inconsistent, highly inconsistent!

It is, of course, much easier to shout, abuse, and howl than to attempt to relate, to explain, to recall *what* Marx and Engels said in 1871, 1872 and 1875 about the experience of the Paris Commune and about the *kind* of state the proletariat needs. . . .

Ex-Marxist Mr. Plekhanov evidently does not care to recall Marxism.

I quoted the words of Rosa Luxemburg, who on August 4, 1914, called *German* Social-Democracy a "stinking corpse." And the Plekhanovs, Goldenbergs and Co. feel "offended." On whose behalf? On behalf of the *German* chauvinists, because they were called chauvinists!

They have got themselves in a mess, these poor Russian social-chauvinists—socialists in word and chauvinists in deed.

36

SIGMUND FREUD

Thoughts for the Times on War and Death

1915

The First World War prompted many leading intellectuals including prominent psychological theorists to develop explanations for why and how the civilized world they inhabited had been transformed into one ravaged by total war. Wartime perspectives from intellectuals such as Sigmund Freud (1856–1939) and Gustave Le Bon (Document 37) demonstrate how new social sciences such as psychology attempted to make sense of the behavior of Europeans confronting modern war. Freud in particular suggested that along with their capacity for rational thought, humans possessed an unconscious mind seething with barely checked desires and emotions.

When war broke out, Freud, a physician and resident of Vienna, in the Austro-Hungarian Empire, had already established an international reputation as the founder of psychoanalysis through the publication of pivotal works such as The Interpretation of Dreams *(1900) and* Five Lectures on Psycho-Analysis *(1910). Freud posited the theory that various unconscious drives toward pleasure and aggression vied with the impulses to repress them, a controversial idea at the time that remains so today. Nonetheless, such thinking had a clear impact on the twentieth century. In this excerpt, Freud offers a psychoanalytic interpretation of World War I in which he stresses that the war had disillusioned those who believed in the progress of civilization and the capacity of humans to regulate their brutal treatment of one another.*

From Sigmund Freud, "Thoughts for the Times on War and Death," in *The Standard Edition of the Complete Psychological Works of Sigmund Freud*, ed. and trans. James Strachey (London: Hogarth Press, 1957), 14:275–80.

In the confusion of wartime in which we are caught up, relying as we must on one-sided information, standing too close to the great changes that have already taken place or are beginning to, and without a glimmering of the future that is being shaped, we ourselves are at a loss as to the significance of the impressions which press in upon us and as to the value of the judgements which we form. We cannot but feel that no event has ever destroyed so much that is precious in the common possessions of humanity, confused so many of the clearest intelligences, or so thoroughly debased what is highest. Science herself has lost her passionless impartiality; her deeply embittered servants seek for weapons from her with which to contribute towards the struggle with the enemy. Anthropologists feel driven to declare him inferior and degenerate, psychiatrists issue a diagnosis of his disease of mind or spirit. Probably, however, our sense of these immediate evils is disproportionately strong, and we are not entitled to compare them with the evils of other times which we have not experienced.

The individual who is not himself a combatant—and so a cog in the gigantic machine of war—feels bewildered in his orientation, and inhibited in his powers and activities. I believe that he will welcome any indication, however slight, which will make it easier for him to find his bearings within himself at least. I propose to pick out two among the factors which are responsible for the mental distress felt by non-combatants, against which it is such a heavy task to struggle, and to treat of them here: the disillusionment which this war has evoked, and the altered attitude towards death which this—like every other war—forces upon us.

When I speak of disillusionment, everyone will know at once what I mean. One need not be a sentimentalist; one may perceive the biological and psychological necessity for suffering in the economy of human life, and yet condemn war both in its means and ends and long for the cessation of all wars. We have told ourselves, no doubt, that wars can never cease so long as nations live under such widely differing conditions, so long as the value of individual life is so variously assessed among them, and so long as the animosities which divide them represent such powerful motive forces in the mind. We were prepared to find that wars between the primitive and the civilized peoples, between the races who are divided by the colour of their skin—wars, even, against and among the nationalities of Europe whose civilization is little developed or has been lost—would occupy mankind for some time to come. But we permitted ourselves to have other hopes. We had expected the great world-dominating nations of white race upon whom the leadership of the human species has fallen, who were known to have world-wide interests as their concern, to whose creative powers were due not only our technical advances towards the control of nature but the artistic and scientific standards of civilization—we had expected these peoples to succeed in discovering another way of settling misunderstandings and conflicts of interest. Within each of these nations high norms of moral conduct were laid down for the individual, to which his manner of life was bound to conform if he desired to take part in a civilized community. These ordinances, often too stringent, demanded a great deal of him—much self-restraint, much renunciation of instinctual satisfaction. He was above all forbidden to make use of the immense advantages to be gained by the practice of lying and deception in the competition with his fellow-men. The civilized states regarded these moral standards as the basis of their existence. They took serious steps if anyone ventured to tamper with them, and often declared it improper even to subject them to examination by a critical intelligence. It was to be assumed, therefore, that the state itself would respect them, and would not think of undertaking anything against them which would contradict the basis of its own existence. Observation showed, to be sure, that embedded in these civilized states there were remnants of certain other peoples, which were universally unpopular and had therefore been only reluctantly, and even so not fully, admitted to participation in the common work of civilization, for which they had shown themselves suitable enough. But the great nations themselves, it might have been supposed, would have acquired so much comprehension of what they had in common, and so much tolerance for their differences, that "foreigner" and "enemy" could no longer be merged, as they still were in classical antiquity, into a single concept. . . .

Then the war in which we had refused to believe broke out, and it brought—disillusionment. Not only is it more bloody and more destructive than any war of other days, because of the enormously increased perfection of weapons of attack and defence; it is at least as cruel, as embittered, as implacable as any that has preceded it. It disregards all the restrictions known as International Law, which in peace-time the states had bound themselves to observe; it ignores the prerogatives of the wounded and the medical service, the distinction between civil and military sections of the population, the claims of private property. It tramples in blind fury on all that comes in its way, as though there were to be no future and no peace among men after it is over. It cuts all the common bonds between the contending peoples, and threatens to leave a legacy of embitterment that will make any renewal of those bonds impossible for a long time to come. . . .

Two things in this war have aroused our sense of disillusionment: the low morality shown externally by states which in their internal relations pose as the guardians of moral standards, and the brutality shown by individuals whom, as participants in the highest human civilization, one would not have thought capable of such behaviour.

37

GUSTAVE LE BON

The Psychology of the Great War

1916

Like Sigmund Freud (Document 36), the French thinker Gustave Le Bon (1841–1931) was trained as a physician. He became well known for his psychological and sociological studies, most famously Psychologie des Foules *(*The Psychology of Crowds*) (1895), in which he argued that the collective mind of the crowd can subordinate the will of an individual. If we link the ideas of Freud to those of Le Bon, when the masses' instincts for death overwhelm their instincts for pleasure, they can be mobilized for war. These masses—which so many middle-class political and social commentators in the late nineteenth and early twentieth centuries, including Le Bon, had come to fear—can then become dedicated to a larger cause and channel their energy into greater and potentially destabilizing political activities. In this study of the psychology of total war, Le Bon addresses the effect that war has on both individual and collective behavior. He argues that war brings forth a renewal of patriotic and religious feelings and, most significantly, that a collective, national will emerges that is greater than the sum of its parts.*

From Gustave Le Bon, *The Psychology of the Great War*, trans. E. Andrews (New York: Macmillan, 1916), 31–32, 304–7, 311–12.

The Collective Forces

The mentality of men in crowds is absolutely unlike that which they possess when isolated, for an assemblage of men is as different from the individuals of whom it is made up as is any living being from its component cells.

Reason has very little influence upon the collective mind, which is governed by collective logic, a form strictly peculiar to it. Intellectually collective man always appears inferior to individual man, but may be superior to him in the domain of the feelings; for although certain feelings, like gratitude, for instance, are unknown to the crowd, it possesses others, such as altruism, devotion to the general welfare, and even heroism, which are far more difficult to put in practice. The powers of the average man are increased by joining a collectivity, while those of the superior man are curtailed.

The emotions of the crowd are both intense and fickle, thus allowing it to change quickly from adoration to hatred, and as it is lacking in the sense of practical possibilities, hope is its principal nourishment. The mysticism with which it is impregnated induces it to attribute magic powers to the leader who beguiles it, and to the brief formulas which synthesize its desires. Mental contagion operates upon isolated individuals as well as upon collectivities, but as the latter do not reason it plays the leading part among them.

The crowd is likewise very receptive of illusions, which acquire the force of truths from the mere fact of becoming collective. The present war furnishes numerous examples of this law.

Collective opinion has a great deal of strength, which is seldom spontaneous, however, for the crowd is really an amorphous organism that is incapable of action unless it has a leader, who influences it by affirmation, repetition, prestige, and contagion, all of them methods of persuasion peculiar to affective logic.

There must always be a leader to create and direct public opinion, even in the case of national conflicts, though this leader need not be a man who harangues the crowd, for his part may be played by beliefs or inherited feelings which certain circumstances have violently inflamed. . . .

The Emergence of New Personalities

A prolonged war, like the one which is causing the present upheaval in Europe, is one of those fundamental events that have the power to alter the equilibrium of the elements which compose our mental life. . . .

Changes of this sort come about as instantaneously as the events which produce them. At a time when luxury and love of comfort seemed to have made a life of danger and privation an impossibility, hundreds of thousands of men, who were in no wise prepared to confront the daily menace of a terrible death, have become as brave as the most famous warriors of olden days. Heroism is a commonplace to them, and when one reads the list of those mentioned in dispatches one sees that persons whose callings in civil life are all that is peaceful give proof of boundless intrepidity upon the field of battle.

The present war is, therefore, one more justification of the theory already presented in my other books, that the apparent persistence of personality simply results from persistence of environment. The man whom we know in every-day life may change until he is unrecognizable, for each one of us has various possibilities of character which emerge in different ways under the pressure of circumstances. Therefore nobody can maintain that he knows himself.

All spectators are impressed with the profound changes in mentality exhibited by members of the various social classes which make up the army, and as one of them says: —

"A peculiar mentality has developed among our soldiers, whom circumstances often carry to heroic heights. They sacrifice themselves willingly, are unselfish and filled with enthusiasm, but unnecessary talk is repugnant to them. Gabblers are not tolerated in the firing-line, for the Frenchman is no longer to be caught with fair words. But to make up for this there is so much solidarity between the men that when some dangerous surprise attack is ordered there is no need to ask for volunteers, since every one is ready to offer himself. Duty and warfare have ennobled every soldier. An officer of my acquaintance was once a Trappist, and the men whom he commands were not at all well behaved in Paris, but they are excellent soldiers now, and in the eyes of their comrades their past errors are already redeemed" (*Le Temps*, July 27, 1915).

This new mentality implies the development of certain feelings, the chief of which I shall now point out.

Exaltation of Patriotism. Influence Exerted by the Spirit of the Race

Love of one's country, or patriotism, necessitates the complete sacrifice of personal interest to the general interest. As the spirit of the race becomes increasingly stabilized by centuries of life and interests in common, patriotism grows stronger, for the instinct of collective conservation is then easily substituted for that of individual conservation.

The spirit of the race is the real combatant in war, and the more its existence is threatened the more vigorously it defends itself. Patriotism is an inherited quality of a mystic, not of a rational, nature, for any one who is a patriot by virtue of reason alone is a poor patriot, and his patriotism does not last long. . . .

Patriotism, the heritage of the dead, is one of those supreme forces which are created by long ancestral accumulations, and whose strength is revealed at critical moments. It was patriotism which rallied to its banner on the very day war was declared the Pacifists, Syndicalists, Socialists, and others who belonged to parties that were apparently most refractory to its influence; nor could their unanimous support have been won had patriotism not been an unconscious force whose impetus swept every argument aside. . . .

Development of Popular Feeling during the War

It is difficult to speak about the development of popular feeling during the war, for although there are evident changes of feeling and thought in every social stratum, the forms which they will ultimately assume are still unknown.

Whether the struggle is to stop or be carried on will be decided in great part by the development of public opinion in the different countries involved, for what things really are is a much less important matter than what one thinks about them, and he who believes in his own defeat will soon see it come to pass. At present the world is ruled by collective concepts, whose formation is slow, but whose force is irresistible when they have acquired their full growth. This is why Germany has made so many efforts to win public opinion; but she has distorted the truth so often that people could not continue to believe in her statements. Her mystic conviction of her triumph has not weakened yet, however, nor will it do so until she feels that the God of Battles is forsaking her.

38

G. ELLIOT SMITH AND T. H. PEAR

Shell Shock and Its Lessons

1917

By 1917, when this small volume appeared, physicians such as Grafton Elliot Smith (1871–1937) and Tom Hatherley Pear (1886–1972), both associated with the University of Manchester in England, had begun to assess the appearance of a seemingly new malady that affected combatants. As the name shell shock *implies, doctors examining soldiers who exhibited a variety of neurological and psychological ailments—for example, the inability to hear, speak, see, or move when there was no physical cause for such symptoms—attributed them initially to the brain damage caused by proximity to exploding shells. By the middle of the war, the term* shell shock *had stuck, even though some soldiers exhibiting such psychosomatic disorders had had no exposure to artillery fire. Unlike works by Sigmund Freud (Document 36) and Gustave Le Bon (Document 37), this volume was an exercise in more practical psychology, detailing the symptoms and treatment for combatants suffering from a variety of war-induced trauma, and revealing the limits, as well as the determination, of the medical community to understand and treat this illness, whatever its cause.*

Although the term shell-shock has been applied to a group of affections, many of which cannot strictly be designated as "shock," and into the causation of which the effect of the explosion of shells is merely one of many exciting factors, this term has now come to possess a more or less definite significance in official documents and in current conversation. It is for this reason that we have chosen to use it rather than the more satisfactory, but less widely employed term, "War-Strain." The reader will, therefore, understand that whenever the term shell-shock appears in these pages, it is to be understood as a popular but inadequate title for

---

From G. Elliot Smith and T. H. Pear, *Shell Shock and Its Lessons*, 2nd ed. (Manchester, U.K.: Manchester University Press, 1917), 1–3, 8–12.

all those mental effects of war experience which are sufficient to incapacitate a man from the performance of his military duties. The term is vague; perhaps its use implies too much; but this is not altogether a disadvantage, for never in the history of mankind have the stresses and strains laid upon body and mind been so great or so numerous as in the present war. We may therefore expect to find many cases which present not a single disease, not even a mixture, but a chemical compound of diseases, so to speak. In civil life, we often meet with cases of nervous breakdown uncomplicated by any gross physical injury. We are scarcely likely, for example, to meet it complicated by gas poisoning and a bullet wound. Yet such combinations as these—or worse—are to be met with in the hospitals every day.

This is perhaps an opportune place to point out a significant popular misunderstanding concerning the nature of such maladies as we shall discuss in this chapter. A common way of describing the condition of a man sent back with "shock" is to say that he has "lost his reason" or "lost his senses." As a rule, this is a singularly inapt description of such a condition. Whatever may be the state of mind of the patient immediately after the mine explosion, the burial in the dug-out, the sight and sound of his lacerated comrades, or other appalling experiences which finally incapacitate him for service in the firing line, it is true to say that by the time of his arrival in a hospital in England his reason and his senses are usually not lost but functioning with painful efficiency.

His reason tells him quite correctly, and far too often for his personal comfort, that had he not given, or failed to carry out, a particular order, certain disastrous and memory-haunting results might not have happened. It tells him, quite convincingly, that in his present state he is not as other men are. Again, the patient reasons, quite logically, but often from false premises, that since he is showing certain symptoms which he has always been taught to associate with "madmen," he is mad too, or on the way to insanity. If nobody is available to receive this man's confidence, to knock away the false foundations of his belief, to bring the whole structure of his nightmare clattering about his ears, and finally, to help him to rebuild for himself (not merely to reconstruct for him) a new and enlightened outlook on his future—in short, if he is left alone, told to "cheer up" or unwisely isolated, it may be his reason, rather than the lack of it, which will prove to be his enemy. And nobody who has observed the hyperæsthesia to noises and light in the nerve-hospital, nobody who has seen the effects upon the patients of a coal dropping unexpectedly out of the fire, will have much respect for the phrase, "lost his senses." There exist, of course, cases of functional blindness,

deafness, cutaneous anæsthesia and the rest, but the majority of the nerve patients show none of these disorders and recovery from them is often rapid.

In a word, it is not in the intellectual but in the *emotional* sphere that we must look for terms to describe these conditions. These disturbances are characterised by instability and exaggeration of emotion rather than by ineffective or impaired reason. And as we shall see later, in the re-education of the patient, the physician is compelled continually to take this fact into account. . . .

It must be understood that this suppression of the external manifestations of an emotion such as fear is but a partial dominance of the bodily concomitants of that emotion. The only changes which can usually be controlled by the will are those of the voluntary or skeletal muscular system, not those of the involuntary or visceral mechanism. While no signs of fear can yet be detected in the face, the body, limbs or voice, these disturbances of the respiratory, circulatory, digestive and excretory systems may be present in a very unpleasant degree, probably even intensified because the nervous energy is denied other channels of outlet.

The suppression of fear and other strong emotions is not demanded only of men in the trenches. It is constantly expected in ordinary society. But the experience of the war has brought two facts prominently before us. First, before this epoch of trench warfare very few people have been called upon to suppress fear continually for a very long period of time. Secondly, men feel fear in different ways and in very various degrees. . . .

The impossibility of regarding modern methods of warfare in the same light as natural and primitive means of fighting appears very clearly when we consider the instinctive and emotional factors involved in the two sets of circumstances. In natural fighting, face to face with his antagonist, and armed only with his hands or with some primitive weapon for close fighting, the uppermost instinct in a healthy man would naturally be that of pugnacity, with its accompanying emotion of anger. The effect of every blow would be visible, and the intense excitement aroused in the relatively short contest would tend to obliterate the action of other instincts such as that of flight, with its emotion of fear. But in trench warfare the conditions are different. A man has seldom a personal enemy whom he can see and upon whom he can observe the effects of his attacks. His anger cannot be directed intensely night and day against a trench full of unseen men in the same way in which it can be provoked by an attack upon him by an individual. And frequently the assaults made upon him nowadays are impersonal, undiscriminating and unpredictable, as in the case of heavy shelling. One natural way is forbidden him in which he might give vent to his pent-up emotion, by rushing out and charging the enemy. He is thus attacked from within and without. The noise of the bursting shells, the premonitory sounds of approaching missiles during exciting periods of waiting, and the sight of those injured in his vicinity whom he cannot help, all assail him, while at the same time he may be fighting desperately with himself. Finally, he may collapse when a shell bursts near him, though he need not necessarily have been injured by actual contact with particles of the bursting missile, earth thrown up by its impact, or gases emanating from its explosion. He may or may not be rendered unconscious at the time. He is removed from the trenches with loss of consciousness or in a dazed or delirious condition with twitchings, tremblings or absence of muscular power.

Upon recovery of consciousness, which may take place after periods varying between a few minutes and a few weeks, the immediate disorders of sensation, emotion, intellect, and movement, are often very severe. It may be presumed that at the beginning of the war they must have appeared far more serious to most of the doctors who saw them in their early stages than they would now. This speculation is suggested by the evidence of the case-sheets sent with the men from France in the early period of the campaign. Such diagnoses as "delusional insanity," and other similar terms taken from the current classifications of advanced conditions of insanity, appear very frequently as descriptions of cases which on arrival in England had almost entirely lost every sign of mental unusualness. In fact, one of the most cheering aspects of work amongst this type of case has been the rapidity with which men who have presented quite alarming symptoms have subsequently recovered. . . .

The most obvious phenomena are undoubtedly the disturbances of sensation and movement. A soldier may be struck blind, deaf or dumb by a bursting shell: in rare cases he may exhibit all three disorders simultaneously or even successively. It should be added that these troubles often vanish after a short space of time, as suddenly and dramatically as they appeared. Thus one of the blinded soldier survivors of the *Hesperian* recovered his sight on being thrown into the water. Other blind patients have had their sight restored under the action of hypnosis. Mutism is often conquered by the shock of a violent emotion, produced accidentally or purposely. Examples of such "shocking" events taken at random from our experience were the sight of another patient slipping from the arms of an orderly, the "going under" chloroform, the application of a faradic current to the neck, the announcement at a "picture house" of Rumania's entry into the war (this cured two cases simultaneously), and the sight of the antics of our most popular film comedian. The latter agency cured a case of functional deaf-mutism, the patient's first auditory sensations being the sound of his own laugh.

Poetic Responses after Years of War

39

EDITH SITWELL

The Dancers

1918

Late in the conflict, the unity that states had demanded of all their inhabitants in order to wage war fragmented. This led not only to revolution and political protests over shortages at home and the direction of the war, but also to attacks on civilians for living easily while the men-at-arms suffered. Many such criticisms came from soldiers who had harsh things to say about "shirkers" and spoiled women war workers living in luxury from their high wages. Civilians could also be critical of one another. In this poem, the innovative British writer Edith Sitwell (1887–1964) contrasts the battlefields with the dance floor, critiquing noncombatants' capacity to indulge in a dance while others died for them.

(During a great battle, 1916).

The floors are slippery with blood:
The world gyrates too. God is good
That while His wind blows out the light
For those who hourly die for us—
We still can dance, each night.

Edith Sitwell, "The Dancers," in *Clowns' Houses* (Oxford: Blackwell, 1918), 25.

The music has grown numb with death —
But we will suck their dying breath,
The whispered name they breathed to chance,
To swell our music, make it loud
That we may dance, — may dance.

We are the dull blind carrion-fly
That dance and batten. Though God die
Mad from the horror of the light —
The light is mad, too, flecked with blood, —
We dance, we dance, each night.

40

WILFRED OWEN

Dulce et Decorum Est

October 1917–March 1918

This poem may be the most famous literary representation of the First World War in the English language, but it was largely unknown during the war itself. An officer killed in the line of duty at the very end of the war, the English poet Wilfred Owen (1893–1918) enlisted in October 1915 and went to fight in France at the end of 1916. He spent some time being treated for shell shock in 1917 before returning to the western front in 1918. Although some of his work appeared in print during the war (including pieces in the journal Wheels, *founded by Edith Sitwell [Document 39] and her brothers), Owen largely achieved posthumous fame. In his poems, scribbled at times while he was in the trenches and later reworked, Owen expressed the suffering and points of connection across no-man's-land, the divide between enemies, and the gap between the older generation of men telling "the old Lie" of patriotism, glory, and duty and the young men who then died horrifically for their nation and their comrades. The Latin words concluding the poem translate to: "It is sweet and honorable to die for one's country."*

Wilfred Owen, "Dulce et Decorum Est," in *Poems by Wilfred Owen* (New York: Viking Press, 1921), 15.

Bent double, like old beggars under sacks,
Knock-kneed, coughing like hags, we cursed through sludge,
Till on the haunting flares we turned our backs,
And towards our distant rest began to trudge.
Men marched asleep. Many had lost their boots,
But limped on, blood-shod. All went lame, all blind;
Drunk with fatigue; deaf even to the hoots
Of gas-shells dropping softly behind.

Gas!, GAS!, Quick, boys!—An ecstasy of fumbling,
Fitting the clumsy helmets just in time,
But someone still was yelling out and stumbling
And flound'ring like a man in fire or lime.—
Dim through the misty panes and thick green light,
As under a green sea, I saw him drowning.

In all my dreams before my helpless sight
He plunges at me, guttering, choking, drowning.

If in some smothering dreams, you too could pace
Behind the wagon that we flung him in,
And watch the white eyes writhing in his face,
His hanging face, like a devil's sick of sin,
If you could hear, at every jolt, the blood
Come gargling from the froth-corrupted lungs
Bitten as the cud[1]
Of vile, incurable sores on innocent tongues,—
My friend, you would not tell with such high zest
To children ardent for some desperate glory,
The old Lie: *Dulce et decorum est*
Pro patria mori.

---

[1] Subsequent printings of this poem usually include a variation on this line, reading "Obscene as a cancer, bitter as the cud."

3

The Aftermath of the First World War

41

THE TIMES OF LONDON

Casualties in the World War

1914–1918

In the war's immediate aftermath, the Times *of London published this official accounting of the war's military casualties. The list was broken down into categories listing the dead, missing, and wounded. Missing from this tally is a broader context, such as placing these statistics in terms of the population mobilized as a percentage of the total population. Nor does the chart break down the numbers according to the battle zones in which the casualties occurred.*

Numbers alone clearly cannot capture the enormity of the war's losses. While it may be helpful to recognize that France lost a greater proportion of its population than did Germany, this alone *fails to explain the war's effects in either state. Using this table as a starting point, we might find it useful to remind ourselves that behind each death or casualty were families, friends, and communities left to mourn or to cope with the shattered lives that injured men had to rebuild, and that some could not.*

"Appendix 1: Casualties in the World War, 1914–1918," in *The* Times *Diary and Index of the War, 1914–1918* (London: The Times, 1919).

Casualties in the World-War, 1914–1918[1]

COUNTRY	DEAD	MISSING, &C	WOUNDED	TOTALS
America	107,284	4,912	191,000	303,196
Austria	687,534	855,283	2,500,000	4,042,817
Belgium	267,000	10,000	140,000	417,000
Britain	851,117	142,057	2,067,442	2,960,616
Bulgaria	101,224	10,825	1,152,399	1,264,448
France	1,039,600	245,900	2,560,000	3,845,500
Germany	1,600,000	721,000	4,064,000	6,385,000
Greece	15,000	45,000	40,000	100,000
Italy	462,391	569,216	953,886	4,385,487
Japan	300	3	907	1,210
Portugal	8,367			
Rumania	332,000	116,000	200,000	648,000
Russia	1,700,000	2,500,000	4,950,000	9,150,000
Serbia	707,343	100,000	350,000	1,157,343
Turkey	436,974	103,731	407,772	948,477

[1] To help put some of this data in context, here are the total numbers of men mobilized in the main participant states relative to the total population: Austria-Hungary, 7.80 million (49.90 million); Belgium, 0.27 million (7.52 million); France, 8.66 million (39.60 million); Germany, 13.40 million (67 million); Italy, 5.90 million (35 million); Russia, 12 million (167 million); Serbia, 0.71 million (5 million); Turkey, 0.99 million (21.30 million); United Kingdom, 5.70 million (46.40 million); and United States, 4.35 million (92 million). *Source:* From John Ellis and Michael Cox, *The World War I Databook* (London: Aurum Press, 2001), table 6.1, 270.

42

CHICAGO DAILY TRIBUNE

America First, Now and Hereafter

January 13, 1918

On January 8, 1918, President Woodrow Wilson addressed the U.S. Congress to outline a proposal for a lasting peace in the aftermath of the First World War. Months before the United States would enter the war, this speech listed fourteen points that should govern the postwar settlement, ranging from broad statements of principles to specific details about territory. Wilson's proposal, which came to be called the "Fourteen Points," helped set the framework for the negotiations that would follow the conclusion of the fighting and articulated a vision of a postwar international order that would value "open covenants of peace, openly arrived at" (an end to secret treaties) and most important, would create "a general association of nations . . . for the purpose of affording mutual guarantees of political independence and territorial integrity to great and small states alike." The reaction to the speech in the United States was swift and, as the editorial in the Republican-leaning Chicago Daily Tribune *reveals, not entirely favorable. The criticism that Wilson's ideas were too idealistic and sacrificed too much of America's own stature foreshadowed the U.S. Senate's later rejection of the Treaty of Versailles. It also reflected the values of the Republican opposition to the Democrat Wilson and to his vision of internationalism. The United States' refusal to participate in the League of Nations after the war weakened that body and helped ensure that Wilson's dream of a general association of nations wielding power to preserve justice and peace could not succeed.*

President Wilson's statement of immediate war aims unifies and points national effort. No one could have declared them better. Lloyd George did not. The president showed a more sympathetic understanding of democratic impulses. Mr. Wilson may win Russia. Lloyd George discarded it, not with petulance but with regret. With respect to Russia Mr. Wilson proved himself the greater statesman.

"America First, Now and Hereafter," editorial, *Chicago Daily Tribune,* January 13, 1918, D4.

Admiration of Mr. Wilson, however, turns to apprehension when he turns from the immediate to the obscure future. Frankly, we dread the effect of his ideas upon the United States. We do not wish the United States to become the kind of a nation it would become if his ideas became effective.

The altruistic beauty of his scheme of life may be radiant and glorious. We do not like it. An intense American, proud, hopeful, aspiring, ambitious for American dignity, power, and greatness, to be achieved in justness and fairness, could not like it.

An intense American wants the United States to be itself, strong in its own right, not in its dependence upon agreements; secure by the efforts of its own people, not by the good will of others; integrated by its devotion to its own principles, traditions, ideals, not disintegrated by the diffusion of its thought and the laxness of its hold upon its people.

Intense nationalism, we hold, is a precious possession to be wished imperishable. It is a leaven in human motives, a sanctuary in human thoughts, an intangible beauty in much tangible ugliness, a force in human development and production.

Mr. Wilson in his search for the altruistic good of the human race is, in a fashion we dread, antinationalistic. It is not right for a great leader to be swept off his feet even by horror of so malevolent a thing as this war or by vision of a greater good. It is bad for emotion to take the place of calculation.

In dealing with the obscure future Mr. Wilson was in places explicit and in places not. Neither in Washington nor in London nor elsewhere is it understood precisely what he meant by the removal of economic barriers and the establishment of equality of trade conditions. We may assume that this is in the president's scheme of internationalism as it was in Richard Cobden's,[1] a factor to guarantee the stability of the international judiciary, the permanence of disarmament, and the continuance of peace.

We might question the propriety of raising so serious a domestic issue as free trade in the midst of a foreign war and of stipulating that American peace commissioners will be instructed to put this domestic legislation in an international agreement in any form whatever. Mr. Wilson may not mean that. We are certain that, regardless of specifications, what he does mean is to use the economic factor so far as possible in breaking down nationalistic competition, and for the good of the United States nationalistic competition is precisely what we want to retain.

---

[1]Cobden (1804–1865) was a British Liberal politician and social reformer.

We do not know what he means by his description of freedom of the seas, but when the British acclaim his proposal we know that they find in it a means of preserving British naval superiority. Whatever be the form of words to cover this or the scheme by which they are made effective if the British accept them or it, we may know that the security of the British kingdom and empire is protected by the British fleet. This, until an American fleet shall assume that superiority, is as Americans must wish it to be. If any foreign fleet shall control the sea we prefer it to be the British, whose method of control we know. But we do not want to subordinate the American navy to the position of a policeman on a beat.

Mr. Wilson would make the military forces of the United States, as of all nations, merely constabulary, maintained for the domestic security and thus, in the worst form of national military organization, detested by the classes against which it might be used, favored by the classes which might use it, a factor in the stratifying of a nation, of arraying class against class.

We want the army of the United States to be civilian, to be integrating, nationalizing, of all classes, equalizing, an instrument of social discipline, of instruction in national responsibility, and a permanent institution of American safety.

The program of intense Americanism is nationalizing. The program of Mr. Wilson is denationalizing. THE TRIBUNE is not opposed to any measures or plans which aim to bring nations into agreement and which are designed to preserve peace unless such measures and plans threaten the nationality of the United States.

We fear that the drift of the American government now, whether consciously or unconsciously, is denationalizing. For that reason we dread it and shall oppose it. It springs to internationalizing schemes. It shuns nationalizing plans. It preaches international altruism. It does not emphasize national integration.

Intense Americanism cannot rejoice in this. We cannot observe other than with dismay the progress of an idea insistently international when the right of Americans to the development of that most precious possession, their sacramental nationality, is being ignored.

43

The Treaty of Versailles

June 28, 1919

After nearly six months of negotiations among the four leaders of the Allied powers—President Woodrow Wilson of the United States, Prime Minister David Lloyd George of Great Britain, Premier Georges Clemenceau of France, and Prime Minister Vittorio Orlando of Italy—and legions of diplomats, the Treaty of Versailles was signed on June 28, 1919. This treaty was the major peace settlement of the war in terms of the Allies' main opponent, Germany. It was the most significant but not the only treaty to end the war; separate treaties were signed with Austria in 1919 and Hungary in 1920, and the Treaties of Sèvres and Lausanne concluded the peace with the Ottoman Empire in the early 1920s.

Prior to America's entry into the war, Wilson had announced his aims for a "non-punitive" peace as part of his Fourteen Points. This goal went unrealized, as the treaty instead forced Germany to accept all responsibility for causing the war and to pay reparations as a result. In addition, the treaty greatly reduced Germany's military strength. The Austro-Hungarian and German empires, including the territories that Russia had ceded to Germany in the Treaty of Brest-Litovsk in March 1918, gave way to a host of new, independent states in central Europe. The postwar settlement further punished Germany by taking away its overseas empire and giving new possessions to Britain, France, and Japan; these included mandates under the League of Nations, also created by the treaty. In these excerpts from the treaty, we can see some of the key features of this document—sometimes deemed the "peace to end all peace."

THE HIGH CONTRACTING PARTIES,

In order to promote international co-operation and to achieve international peace and security

by the acceptance of obligations not to resort to war,
by the prescription of open, just and honourable relations between nations,

---

From *The Treaty of Peace and the Covenant of the League of Nations* (Philadelphia: John C. Winston, 1920), 43–46, 54–57, 104, 217–18.

by the firm establishment of the understandings of international law as the actual rule of conduct among Governments, and

by the maintenance of justice and a scrupulous respect for all treaty obligations in the dealings of organised peoples with one another,

Agree to this Covenant of the League of Nations.

Article 1. The original Members of the League of Nations shall be those of the Signatories which are named in the Annex to this Covenant and also such of those other States named in the Annex as shall accede without reservation to this Covenant. Such accession shall be effected by a Declaration deposited with the Secretariat within two months of the coming into force of the Covenant. Notice thereof shall be sent to all other Members of the League.

Any fully self-governing State, Dominion or Colony not named in the Annex may become a Member of the League if its admission is agreed to by two-thirds of the Assembly, provided that it shall give effective guarantees of its sincere intention to observe its international obligations, and shall accept such regulations as may be prescribed by the League in regard to its military, naval and air forces and armaments.

Any Member of the League may, after two years' notice of its intention so to do, withdraw from the League, provided that all its international obligations and all its obligations under this Covenant shall have been fulfilled at the time of its withdrawal. . . .

Article 4. The Council shall consist of Representatives of the Principal Allied and Associated Powers, together with Representatives of four other Members of the League. These four Members of the League shall be selected by the Assembly from time to time in its discretion. Until the appointment of the Representatives of the four Members of the League first selected by the Assembly, Representatives of Belgium, Brazil, Spain and Greece shall be members of the Council.

With the approval of the majority of the Assembly, the Council may name additional Members of the League whose Representatives shall always be members of the Council; the Council with like approval may increase the number of Members of the League to be selected by the Assembly for representation on the Council.

The Council shall meet from time to time as occasion may require, and at least once a year, at the Seat of the League, or at such other place as may be decided upon.

The Council may deal at its meetings with any matter within the sphere of action of the League or affecting the peace of the world.

Any Member of the League not represented on the Council shall be invited to send a Representative to sit as a member at any meeting of the Council during the consideration of matters specially affecting the interests of that Member of the League.

At meetings of the Council, each Member of the League represented on the Council shall have one vote, and may have not more than one Representative.

Article 5. Except where otherwise expressly provided in this Covenant or by the terms of the present Treaty, decisions at any meeting of the Assembly or of the Council shall require the agreement of all the Members of the League represented at the meeting.

All matters of procedure at meetings of the Assembly or of the Council, including the appointment of Committees to investigate particular matters, shall be regulated by the Assembly or by the Council and may be decided by a majority of the Members of the League represented at the meeting.

The first meeting of the Assembly and the first meeting of the Council shall be summoned by the President of the United States of America. . . .

Article 22. To those colonies and territories which as a consequence of the late war have ceased to be under the sovereignty of the States which formerly governed them and which are inhabited by peoples not yet able to stand by themselves under the strenuous conditions of the modern world, there should be applied the principle that the well-being and development of such peoples form a sacred trust of civilisation and that securities for the performance of this trust should be embodied in this Covenant.

The best method of giving practical effect to this principle is that the tutelage of such peoples should be entrusted to advanced nations who by reason of their resources, their experience or their geographical position can best undertake this responsibility, and who are willing to accept it, and that this tutelage should be exercised by them as Mandatories on behalf of the League.

The character of the mandate must differ according to the stage of the development of the people, the geographical situation of the territory, its economic conditions and other similar circumstances.

Certain communities formerly belonging to the Turkish Empire have reached a stage of development where their existence as independent nations can be provisionally recognised subject to the rendering of administrative advice and assistance by a Mandatory until such time as they are able to stand alone. The wishes of these communities must be a principal consideration in the selection of the Mandatory.

Other peoples, especially those of Central Africa, are at such a stage that the Mandatory must be responsible for the administration of the territory under conditions which will guarantee freedom of conscience and religion, subject only to the maintenance of public order and morals, the prohibition of abuses such as the slave trade, the arms traffic and the liquor traffic, and the prevention of the establishment of fortifications or military and naval bases and of military training of the natives for other than police purposes and the defence of territory, and will also secure equal opportunities for the trade and commerce of other Members of the League.

There are territories, such as South-West Africa and certain of the South Pacific Islands, which, owing to the sparseness of their population, or their small size, or their remoteness from the centres of civilisation, or their geographical contiguity to the territory of the Mandatory, and other circumstances, can be best administered under the laws of the Mandatory as integral portions of its territory, subject to the safeguards above mentioned in the interests of the indigenous population.

In every case of mandate, the Mandatory shall render to the Council an annual report in reference to the territory committed to its charge.

The degree of authority, control, or administration to be exercised by the Mandatory shall, if not previously agreed upon by the Members of the League, be explicitly defined in each case by the Council.

A permanent Commission shall be constituted to receive and examine the annual reports of the Mandatories and to advise the Council on all matters relating to the observance of the mandates.

Article 23.   Subject to and in accordance with the provisions of international conventions existing or hereafter to be agreed upon, the Members of the League:

   (*a*)   will endeavour to secure and maintain fair and humane conditions of labour for men, women, and children, both in their own countries and in all countries to which their commercial and industrial relations extend, and for that purpose will establish and maintain the necessary international organisations;

(*b*) undertake to secure just treatment of the native inhabitants of territories under their control;

(*c*) will entrust the League with the general supervision over the execution of agreements with regard to the traffic in women and children, and the traffic in opium and other dangerous drugs;

(*d*) will entrust the League with the general supervision of the trade in arms and ammunition with the countries in which the control of this traffic is necessary in the common interest;

(*e*) will make provision to secure and maintain freedom of communications and of transit and equitable treatment for the commerce of all Members of the League. In this connection, the special necessities of the regions devastated during the war of 1914–1918 shall be borne in mind;

(*f*) will endeavour to take steps in matters of international concern for the prevention and control of disease. . . .

Article 119. Germany renounces in favour of the Principal Allied and Associated Powers all her rights and titles over her oversea possessions. . . .

Article 231. The Allied and Associated Governments affirm and Germany accepts the responsibility of Germany and her allies for causing all the loss and damage to which the Allied and Associated Governments and their nationals have been subjected as a consequence of the war imposed upon them by the aggression of Germany and her allies. . . .

Article 428. As a guarantee for the execution of the present Treaty by Germany, the German territory situated to the west of the Rhine, together with the bridgeheads, will be occupied by Allied and Associated troops for a period of fifteen years from the coming into force of the present Treaty.

44

E. D. MOREL

The Horror on the Rhine

1920

Under the terms of the Treaty of Versailles, the Allies gained the right to station troops in the Rhineland to guarantee the treaty's terms and, in particular, ensure the payment of reparations. The main occupying forces of the Rhineland were French, and they included a significant number of colonial troops. Soon after, these troops were charged with atrocities, particularly acts of sexual violence, reminiscent of accusations against the German occupying forces in Belgium. In 1920, E. D. Morel (1873– 1924), a British politician and activist who had been a vocal critic both of the abuses committed by imperial powers like Belgium in Africa and of the First World War, published a pamphlet highlighting the alleged mistreatment of Germany by French colonial (black) troops. Despite his prior critique of imperialism, Morel used highly racially charged language to claim that outrages by these troops could only lead to a lasting legacy of hate, especially among German men, and the likelihood of future war. Despite colonial troops' service to their imperial states, postwar racism remained a potent force.

The indictment is against French militarism for conscripting the peoples of Africa and thrusting tens of thousands of African conscripts into the heart of Europe.

. . . for quartering tens of thousands of African troops upon European communities in times of peace.

. . . for initiating a policy which is bound to have demoralising effects in Europe.

. . . for initiating a policy which is bound to have incalculable evil consequences in Africa and for Africa. . . .

If this occupation were not accompanied by deplorable social results it would mean that the sexual requirements of tens of thousands of

From E. D. Morel, *The Horror on the Rhine* (London: Union of Democratic Control, August 1920), 8–10, 20–22. Emphasis in original.

Africans, living in an enforced state of celibacy, had (*a*) either mysteriously disappeared or (*b*) could be satisfied with the services of professional prostitutes. Will anyone outside a lunatic asylum uphold the first postulate? . . .

It is obvious, then, that the sexual requirements of the North and West Central African troops which French militarism has thrust upon the Rhineland must continue to exist, and that in the absence of their own women-folk *must be satisfied upon the bodies of white women.* Assuming these requirements to be fully met by professional prostitutes, the French Government would still be responsible for introducing into Europe, and in aggravated form, the seeds of racial hatred and racial prejudice which is so disturbing a feature in the social conditions of the southern States of the American Union. . . .

. . . If the women of the Rhineland are its helpless victims so also are the Africans whom it conscripts. Indeed the peoples of Europe and Africa are all alike its victims, for it is keeping alive the slumbering fires of hate in Europe as nothing else is doing, and it is kindling new fires in the relations of Europe with Africa. . . .

. . . Hell [has been] created west of the Rhine by French militarism. . . .

. . . For no valid reason can be urged in support of French policy in this respect. . . .

. . . Given the fact of an occupation of German territory in time of peace by African troops, conscripted by their white masters from the North African coast to the Congo forests for the purpose of killing white men in Europe, in which task they have been engaged for five years, occurrences of the kind mentioned in this pamphlet, the brothel system, the growth of prostitution, and the general debasement of the population, were alike inevitable. . . .

. . . The question for us is: Are our infant sons to be doomed to a violent and senseless death in manhood because French militarism is sowing the seeds of ineradicable hatreds in Europe? . . . Are we presently to suffer again because German boys are being told to-day: "They obtained our surrender under false pretences. They promised us an honourable peace. . . . When we were helpless they forced us to sign a Treaty which condemned us to death-in-life. They went on starving us for months and months. . . . They piled humiliation upon humiliation on us. . . . But that was not enough. They inflicted upon us the supreme outrage. From the plains and forests, from the valleys and the swamps of Africa they brought tens of thousands of savage men and thrust them upon us."

45

The Sykes-Picot Agreement

1916

One of the consequences of the defeat of several large imperial powers, including the Ottoman Empire, was the redrawing of political boundaries in territory that victors such as France and Britain were eager to control. The 1916 Sykes-Picot Agreement between Britain and France presaged this end by dividing territory in "Arabia" into zones that after the war would be placed under the direct or indirect control of either Britain or France. The shared goal of these imperial states was to divide what would become known as the Middle East into spheres of influence. This arrangement, negotiated for the British by Mark Sykes (1879–1919) and for the French by François Georges Picot (1870–1951), paved the way for the creation of new states out of the territory formerly under Ottoman control. This document and the Balfour Declaration (Document 46) set the stage for the future development of, and future conflict in, the Middle East.

1. That France and Great Britain are prepared to recognize and protect an independent Arab State or a Confederation of Arab States in the areas (A) and (B) marked on the annexed map (*map not reproduced: Ed.*), under the suzerainty of an Arab chief. That in area (A) France, and in area (B) Great Britain, shall have priority of right of enterprise and local loans. That in area (A) France, and in area (B) Great Britain, shall alone supply advisers or foreign functionaries at the request of the Arab State or Confederation of Arab States.

2. That in the blue area France, and in the red area Great Britain, shall be allowed to establish such direct or indirect administration or control as they desire and as they may think fit to arrange with the Arab State or Confederation of Arab States.

3. That in the brown area there shall be established an international administration, the form of which is to be decided upon after consultation with Russia, and subsequently in consultation with the other Allies, and the representatives of the Shereef of Mecca.

From "The Sykes-Picot Agreement, 1916," in *The Arab-Israeli Reader*, ed. Walter Laquer and Barry Rubin (New York: Facts on File, 1985), 13–15.

4. That Great Britain be accorded (1) the ports of Haifa and Acre, (2) guarantee of a given supply of water from the Tigris and Euphrates in area (A) for area (B). His Majesty's Government, on their part, undertake that they will at no time enter into negotiations for the cession of Cyprus to any third Power without the previous consent of the French Government.

5. That Alexandretta shall be a free port as regards the trade of the British Empire, and that there shall be no discrimination in port charges or facilities as regards British shipping and British goods; that there shall be freedom of transit for British goods through Alexandretta and by railway through the blue area, whether those goods are intended for or originate in the red area, or (B) area, or area (A); and there shall be no discrimination, direct or indirect against British goods on any railway or against British goods or ships at any port serving the areas mentioned.

That Haifa shall be a free port as regards the trade of France, her dominions and protectorates, and there shall be no discrimination in port charges or facilities as regards French shipping and French goods. There shall be freedom of transit for French goods through Haifa and by the British railway through the brown area, whether those goods are intended for or originate in the blue area, area (A), or area (B), and there shall be no discrimination, direct or indirect, against French goods on any railway, or against French goods or ships at any port serving the areas mentioned. . . .

9. It shall be agreed that the French Government will at no time enter into any negotiations for the cession of their rights and will not cede such rights in the blue area to any third Power, except the Arab State or Confederation of Arab States without the previous agreement of His Majesty's Government, who, on their part, will give a similar undertaking to the French Government regarding the red area.

10. The British and French Governments, as the protectors of the Arab State, shall agree that they will not themselves acquire and will not consent to a third Power acquiring territorial possessions in the Arabian peninsula, nor consent to a third Power installing a naval base either on the east coast, or on the islands, of the Red Sea. This, however, shall not prevent such adjustment of the Aden frontier as may be necessary in consequence of recent Turkish aggression.

11. The negotiations with the Arabs as to the boundaries of the Arab State or Confederation of Arab States shall be continued through the same channel as heretofore on behalf of the two Powers.

12. It is agreed that measures to control the importation of arms into the Arab territories will be considered by the two Governments.

46

The Balfour Declaration
November 2, 1917

As part of a British strategy to secure its postwar imperial interests in Palestine and in hopes of also hastening the end of the war, the British government sought to find a way to balance its goals with those of other stakeholders in the region. Many in the British government, including Prime Minister David Lloyd George, had come to believe that supporting Zionist interests would provide a counterweight to French ambitions in the area. Some British politicians further hoped that a public declaration of support for a Jewish national homeland in Palestine might encourage Jews in states such as Russia to urge their governments to continue to support the Allies and remain in the war. The 1917 Balfour Declaration, written in the first-person voice of British foreign secretary Arthur James Balfour (1848–1930), committed Britain to support the eventual creation of a Jewish "national home" in Palestine. Balfour addressed his letter to Baron Lionel Walter Rothschild, the most prominent figure in Britain's tiny Jewish community rather than the activists who had campaigned for the measure, but behind the scenes the British government had sought the tacit approval of its allies France, Italy, and the United States regarding its public support of this goal. The declaration was quite vague, was controversial at the time among Jews as well as others, and led to no concrete action in the immediate aftermath of the First World War. Indeed, the intentions expressed in this document remained unrealized until the end of another world war.

FOREIGN OFFICE
NOVEMBER 2ND, 1917.

Dear Lord Rothschild:

I have much pleasure in conveying to you, on behalf of His Majesty's Government, the following declaration of sympathy with Jewish Zionist aspirations which has been submitted to, and approved by, the Cabinet.

From "The Balfour Declaration, 1917," in *The Arab-Israeli Reader*, ed. Walter Laquer and Barry Rubin (New York: Facts on File, 1985), 18.

"His Majesty's Government view with favour the establishment in Palestine of a national home for the Jewish people, and will use their best endeavours to facilitate the achievement of this object, it being clearly understood that nothing shall be done which may prejudice the civil and religious rights of existing non-Jewish communities in Palestine, or the rights and political status enjoyed by Jews in any other country."

I should be grateful if you would bring this declaration to the knowledge of the Zionist Federation.

YOURS SINCERELY,

ARTHUR JAMES BALFOUR.

47

WESTMINSTER GAZETTE

Women and Wages: "Equal Pay for Equal Work"

January 28, 1919

One challenge facing wartime nations was the status of women. Many countries, with the notable exception of France, enfranchised some portion of their female populations after the war. In granting women the right to vote, politicians across Europe used language that emphasized their appreciation of the services women had performed and the sacrifices they had made during the war. The participation of women in the labor force, the nature of women's work, and the amount of money that many women could earn had all changed dramatically. While governments and employers had little difficulty persuading some women to return to their traditional roles in the home and family, other women, out of choice or necessity, did not want to leave the world of waged employment. Reactions to the latter varied, but many public voices condemned them. Here is one British employer's response to working women that questions the notion of "equal pay for equal work." It suggests how much women still had to struggle to achieve equal opportunities, let alone equal rights, in the postwar world.

"Women and Wages: 'Equal Pay for Equal Work'—An Employer's View," *Westminster Gazette*, January 28, 1919, Women's Work Collection Press Cuttings, Imperial War Museum, London.

Mr. W. L. Hichens, chairman of Cammell, Laird, and Co.,[1] gave to a representative of the "Westminster Gazette" his views on "equal pay for equal work"—a subject concerning which already much has been said, and probably more will be necessary in the future.

"Briefly, my view of this matter is that 'equal pay for equal work' seems an extraordinarily good catch phrase, but is very misleading," said Mr. Hichens. "What do you mean by equal pay for equal work? It is conceivable that the work of a V.A.D. [Voluntary Aid Detachment] nurse in France is equal to that of a munition worker in England. In determining the relative pay or reward that a stockbroker or an ice-cream vendor gets no one really considers the question as to how far the work of each is equal or unequal. The problem is determined in quite another way, and the plain fact of the matter is that there are a number of factors which go to determine the problem of wages. There is the question of skill, of responsibility, of danger, of disagreeableness, of supply and demand, and the question of the cost of living.

"In determining the minimum wage the question bulking largest is that of the cost of living, and in dealing with a trade that is mainly in the hands of men the cost of living means how much do a man, his wife, and an average of four children require in order to maintain a reasonable existence. If, on the other hand, the problem under consideration is that of a trade in the hands of men and women, the question is how much does it cost a single woman to maintain a reasonable existence. Man is, and always will be, regarded as the bread-winner and woman as the mother. She is, speaking generally, only in industry until she is married; and her object whilst in industry is—again speaking generally—to support herself. It is, of course, true that many single women in industry have parents or invalid relatives dependent upon them, but that is a factor common both to married and unmarried persons, and no one can contend that the fact of marriage exonerates one from the claims of those who are near to us. Therefore, the problem of equal pay for equal work can never in practice be regarded in isolation from these other factors.

"It is reasonable that, if a man and a woman are working side by side at the same class of work, both should be paid alike. It is also reasonable that the broad consideration should not be forgotten as a general rule that the wage of a man is a family wage and the wage of a woman is not. The effect of establishing rigidly the practice of equal pay for equal work would be to reduce the wages of a man; for nothing would have

[1] A British shipbuilding firm.

been done to increase the production, and the only means of finding the additional wages for a woman would be to take it away from the man. Seeing that it is of the greatest importance that the wages of a married man should be as high as possible, this result is to be deprecated.

"One appears to be on the horns of a dilemma. If, on the one hand, women were paid less than men, there might be a tendency on the part of employers to prefer women, and so drive men into unemployment. If, on the other hand, women were paid the same as men, there would be a tendency to employ men in preference to women, especially in some similar class of work, because the man is a worker all his life, and the woman only until she is married."

48

NAR DIOUF

A Senegalese Veteran's Oral Testimony

1919

The consequences of the war for its veterans varied widely. Few who fought in the war emerged from the conflict unaffected. Historians of the soldiers' experience must rely on written records, either those composed for private consumption, such as diaries and letters, or accounts published in memoirs, autobiographies, and thinly veiled fiction. We have no firsthand information about the vast majority of participants, and this is doubly the case for colonial troops. Hence the extraordinary value of the following excerpt from an oral interview conducted with a Senegalese veteran. His account of how dramatically the war changed his life offers a valuable perspective on one of the war's most potent legacies: its effects on colonial soldiers who fought for their colonizers and returned home with new attitudes toward race and their status as colonial subjects.

From Joe Lunn, *Memoirs of the Maelstrom: A Senegalese Oral History of the First World War* (Portsmouth, N.H.: Heinemann, 1999), 232.

I received many lasting things from the war. I demonstrated my dignity and courage, and [I] won the respect of the people and the [colonial] government. And whenever the people of the village had something to contest [with the French]—and they didn't dare do it [themselves] because they were afraid of them—I used to do it for them. And many times when people had problems with the government, I used to go with my decorations and arrange the situation for [them]. Because whenever the *Tubabs*[1] saw your decorations, they knew that they [were dealing with] a very important person. . . . And I gained this ability—of obtaining justice over a *Tubab*—from the war.

[For example], one day a *Tubab* came here [to the village]—he came from the *service de génie*[2] (he was a kind of doctor)—to make an examination of the people. So he came here, and there was a small boy who was blind. And [the boy] was walking, [but] he couldn't see, and he bumped into the *Tubab*. And the *Tubab* turned and pushed the boy [down]. And when I saw that, I came and said to the *Tubab*: "Why have you pushed this boy? [Can't] you see that he is blind?" And the *Tubab* said: "Oh, *pardon, pardon*. I did not know. I will never do it again, excuse me!" [But] before the war, [no matter what they did], it would not have been possible to do that with a *Tubab*.

[1] Europeans.
[2] Engineering corps.

49

OTTO DIX

Flanders Field

1934–1936

Many wartime and postwar artists drew on the jarring landscapes of the war's western front for inspiration. They depicted stark and disturbing scenes in a variety of art works that owed something to prewar movements and much to new and self-consciously modern ways of seeing brought about in part by the war. In the visual arts as much as in literature, modernism as an artistic movement came into its own; so, too, did its offshoots, such as surrealism and expressionism. Flanders Field, *a shocking work by the German war veteran and artist Otto Dix (1891–1969), was meant partly as an homage to its inspiration, a passage from Henri Barbusse's* Under Fire *(Document 21). Dix was twenty-three when he entered the German army in 1914. He saw action along the western front, including at the Battle of the Somme, before transferring to the eastern front. He worked on* Flanders Field *from 1934 to 1936, after the Nazis came to power in Germany, which had led to his being fired from his position at the Dresden Art Academy. In this depiction of the western front, reality is both evoked—the decaying soldier vividly emerges from the ground once the eye finds the shapes of the helmet and the gun—and distorted. The borders between body and trench dissolve, as they must have done in the field, but they do so in a profoundly disordered and disturbing manner.*

Otto Dix, *Flanders Field*, oil and tempera on canvas, 200 × 250 cm, Staatliche Museen Preußischer Kulturbesitz, Berlin.

50

ERNST JÜNGER

Storm of Steel

1920

German war veteran and author Ernst Jünger (1895–1998) published the first version of Instahlgewitten *(Storm of Steel) in 1920. He would continue to revise the novel, and publish various versions of it, throughout his lifetime. Offering a German perspective of warfare along the western front, Jünger also discussed the impact of waging war against colonial troops in Europe and offered his own critique of the war effort on both sides. Jünger was wounded multiple times during the war, winning the Iron Cross at the Battle of the Somme. In contrast to Henri Barbusse (Document 21) and fellow German veteran Erich Maria Remarque (Document 51), Jünger saw no reason to reject militarism out of hand. He and his work were embraced by right-wing politicians, including leading members of the Nazi party, after the war. After his service in the Second World War, he publicly denounced Nazism.*

The first evening was stormy; heavy rain clattered down on the already flooded terrain. Soon, though, a succession of fine warm days reconciled us to our new place. I enjoyed the splendid landscape, untroubled by the white balls of shrapnel and the jumping cones of shells; in fact, barely noticing them. Each spring marked the beginning of a new year's fighting; intimations of a big offensive were as much part of the season as primroses and pussy-willows. . . .

The front line wound its way through meadowland shaded by little clumps of trees, wearing the fresh green of early spring. It was possible to walk safely in front of and behind the trenches, as many advance positions secured the line. These posts were a thorn in the enemy's side, and some weeks not a night would pass without an attempt to remove the sentries, either by guile or by brute force. . . .

From Ernst Jünger, *Storm of Steel*, trans. Michael Hofmann (New York: Penguin, 2003), 141, 143–44, 146–47, 149–50.

Two platoons manned our sector from the Roman road to the so-called Artillery Trench; a third was at company headquarters, some two hundred yards back, behind a little slope. There Kius and I shared a tiny plank lean-to together, trusting to the incompetence of the British artillery. One side was built into the down-hill slope—the direction the shells would be coming from—while the other three offered their flanks to the enemy. Every day as the morning greetings were wafted up to us, one might have heard a conversation between the occupants of the top and bottom bunks that went roughly like this:

"I say, Ernst, are you awake?"

"Hm?"

"I think they're shooting!"

"Oh, I don't want to get up yet; I'm sure they'll be finished soon."

A quarter of an hour later:

"I say, Oskar!"

"Hm?"

"They seem to be going on for ever today; I thought I heard a shrapnel ball come flying through the wall just now. I think we'd better get up after all. The artillery observer next door seems to have scarpered ages ago!"

We were unwise enough always to take our boots off. By the time we were finished, the British usually were too, and we could sit down at the ridiculously small table, drink our sour, stewed coffee, and light a morning cigar. In the afternoons, we mocked the British gunners by lying out on a tarpaulin and doing some sunbathing. . . .

In the middle of my "pipe dreams," I was startled by a distinct rustling coming from the woods and the meadow. In the presence of the enemy, one's senses are always on the qui vive, and it's a strange thing that one can feel sure, even on the basis of rather ordinary sounds: This is it!

Straight away the nearest sentry came rushing up to me: "Lieutenant, sir, there are seventy British soldiers advancing on the edge of the wood!"

Though somewhat surprised at such a precise count, I hid in the tall grass on the slope, along with four riflemen, to wait and see what happened next. A few seconds later, I saw a group of men flitting across the meadow. As my men leveled their rifles at them, I called down a soft: "Who goes there?" It was NCO Teilengerdes, an experienced warrior from the 2nd, collecting up his excited unit.

The other units quickly arrived. I had them form into a line stretching from the slope to the wood. A minute later, they were standing ready, with fixed bayonets. It couldn't hurt to check the alignment; in such situations, you can't be too pedantic. As I was upbraiding a man who was standing a little back, he replied: "I'm a stretcher-bearer, sir." He had his own rules to follow. Relieved, I ordered the men to advance.

As we strode across the strip of meadow, a hail of shrapnel flew over our heads. The enemy was laying down a dense fire in an attempt to disrupt our communications. Involuntarily, we slipped into a jogtrot, to reach the lee of the hill in front of us.

Suddenly, a dark form arose out of the grass. I tore off a hand-grenade and hurled it in the direction of the figure, with a shout. To my consternation, I saw by the flash of the explosion that it was Teilengerdes, who, unnoticed by me, had somehow run on ahead, and tripped over a wire. Fortunately, he was unhurt. Simultaneously, we heard the sharper reports of British grenades, and the shrapnel fire became unpleasantly concentrated.

Our line melted away, in the direction of the steep slope, which was experiencing heavy fire, while Teilengerders and I and three men stayed put. Suddenly one of them jogged me: "Look, the British!"

Like a vision in a dream, the sight, lit only by falling sparks, of a double line of kneeling figures at the instant in which they rose to advance, etched itself into my eye. I could clearly make out the figure of an officer on the right of the line, giving the command to advance. Friend and foe were paralysed by this sudden, unexpected meeting. Then we turned to flee—the only thing we could do—the enemy, it seemed, still too paralysed to fire at us. . . .

Then we saw something that was a rarity in this war of long-range weapons. Out of the dark brush, a line of figures emerged and stepped on to the open meadow. Five, ten, fifteen, a whole line. Trembling fingers took off safety-catches. A distance of fifty yards, thirty, fifteen . . . Fire! The rifles barked for several minutes. Sparks flew as spurts of lead struck weapons and steel helmets.

Suddenly a shout: "Watch out, left!" A mob of attackers was running towards us from the left, headed by an enormous figure with an out-stretched revolver, and swinging a white club.

"Left section! Left front!"

The men spun round, and welcomed the new arrivals in a standing posture. A few of the enemy, among them their leader, collapsed under the hurriedly fired-off shots, the others vanished, as quickly as they had appeared.

Now was our moment to charge. With fixed bayonets and loud hurrahs, we surged into the little wood. Hand-grenades flew into the tangled undergrowth, and in no time at all we were back in control of our outpost, although admittedly without having come to grips with our elusive foe.

We assembled in an adjacent cornfield and gazed at each other's pale and exhausted faces. The sun had risen radiantly. A lark was ascending, getting on our wicks with its trilling. It was all unreal after that feverishly intent night.

While we handed round our canteens and lit cigarettes, we heard the enemy leaving along the path, with a few loudly lamenting wounded in tow. We even caught a glimpse of them, but not long enough to chase after and finish them off.

I went off to survey the battlefield. From the meadow arose exotic calls and cries for help. The voices were like the noise that frogs make in the grass after a rainstorm. In the tall grass we discovered a line of dead and three wounded who threw themselves at our feet and begged us for mercy. They seemed to be convinced that we would massacre them.

In answer to my question "Quelle nation?"[1] one replied: "Pauvre Rajput!"[2]

So these were Indians we had confronted, who had travelled thousands of miles across the sea, only to give themselves a bloody nose on this god-forsaken piece of earth against the Hanoverian Rifles.

They were delicate, and in a bad way. At such short range, an infantry bullet has an explosive effect. Some of them had been hit a second time as they lay there, and in such a way that the bullets had passed longitudinally, down the length of their bodies. All of them had been hit twice, and a few more than that. We picked them up, and dragged them towards our lines. Since they were screaming like banshees, my men tried to hold their mouths shut and brandished their fists at them, which terrified them still more. One died on the way, but he was still taken along, because there was a reward for every prisoner taken, whether alive or dead. The other two tried to ingratiate themselves with us by calling out repeatedly: "Anglais pas bon!"[3] Why these people spoke French I couldn't quite understand. The whole scene—the mixture of the prisoners' laments and our jubilation—had something primordial about it. This wasn't war; it was ancient history.

[1] "What nation?"
[2] "Poor Rajput!"
[3] "English not good."

51

ERICH MARIA REMARQUE

All Quiet on the Western Front

1928

Ten years after the war's end, a flurry of books appeared retelling the experiences of combat. In 1928, the German veteran Erich Maria Remarque (1898–1970) published a novel that quickly became an international bestseller, ushered in a new era of interest in the First World War, and offered an interpretation of the combatants' war experiences that has come to personify this war. Remarque was born Erich Paul Remark in 1898 and called up for military service toward the end of the war. The name that he selected for himself echoed that of poet Rainer Maria Rilke, and he bestowed his middle name and his mother's maiden name on the protagonist of his deeply autobiographical novel, All Quiet on the Western Front. *Both the novel and the film version that appeared in 1930 decisively shaped how the war was remembered and understood, as the utter waste and indeed betrayal of a young, idealistic generation. In telling the story of Paul Bäumer and his tragic and senseless death on the western front, the novel struck a chord with many veterans and also the generation that succeeded them. In turn, its ultimate antiwar message led to its being denounced and banned by the Nazi leadership that came to power in Germany in 1933, and the Nazi government stripped Remarque of his citizenship in 1938. He immigrated to the United States in 1939, eventually becoming a U.S. citizen in 1947, and died in Switzerland in 1970. Nothing he wrote ever achieved the popularity or influence of his first major novel.*

Another wave of our attack has just come up. A lieutenant is with them. He sees us and yells, "Forward, forward, join in, follow." And the word of command does what all my banging could not. Himmelstoss hears the order, looks round him as if awakened, and follows on.

From Erich Maria Remarque, *All Quiet on the Western Front*, trans. A. W. Wheen (New York: Ballantine Books, 1982), 132–35, 280–83, 293–95.

I come after and watch him go over. Once more he is the smart Himmelstoss of the parade-ground, he has even outstripped the lieutenant and is far ahead.

Bombardment, barrage, curtain-fire, mines, gas, tanks, machine-guns, hand-grenades—words, words, but they hold the horror of the world.

Our faces are encrusted, our thoughts are devastated, we are weary to death; when the attack comes we shall have to strike many of the men with our fists to waken them and make them come with us—our eyes are burnt, our hands are torn, our knees bleed, our elbows are raw.

How long has it been? Weeks—months—years? Only days. We see time pass in the colourless faces of the dying, we cram food into us, we run, we throw, we shoot, we kill, we lie about, we are feeble and spent, and nothing supports us but the knowledge that there are still feebler, still more spent, still more helpless ones there who, with staring eyes, look upon us as gods that escape death many times.

In the few hours of rest we teach them. "There, see that waggle-top? That's a mortar coming. Keep down, it will go clean over. But if it comes this way, then run for it. You can run from a mortar."

We sharpen their ears to the malicious, hardly audible buzz of the smaller shells that are not easily distinguishable. They must pick them out from the general din by their insect-like hum—we explain to them that these are far more dangerous than the big ones that can be heard long beforehand.

We show them how to take cover from aircraft, how to simulate a dead man when one is overrun in an attack, how to time hand-grenades so that they explode half a second before hitting the ground; we teach them to fling themselves into holes as quick as lightning before the shells with instantaneous fuses; we show them how to clean up a trench with a handful of bombs; we explain the difference between the fuse-length of the enemy bombs and our own; we put them wise to the sound of gas shells;—show them all the tricks that can save them from death.

They listen, they are docile—but when it begins again, in their excitement they do everything wrong.

Haie Westhus drags off with a great wound in his back through which the lung pulses at every breath. I can only press his hand; "It's all up, Paul," he groans and he bites his arm because of the pain.

We see men living with their skulls blown open; we see soldiers run with their two feet cut off, they stagger on their splintered stumps into the next shell-hole; a lance-corporal crawls a mile and a half on his hands dragging his smashed knee after him; another goes to the dressing station and over his clasped hands bulge his intestines; we see men without mouths, without jaws, without faces; we find one man who has held the artery of his arm in his teeth for two hours in order not to bleed to death. The sun goes down, night comes, the shells whine, life is at an end.

Still the little piece of convulsed earth in which we lie is held. We have yielded no more than a few hundred yards of it as a prize to the enemy. But on every yard there lies a dead man.

* * *

. . . We are emaciated and starved. Our food is bad and mixed up with so much substitute stuff that it makes us ill. The factory owners in Germany have grown wealthy;—dysentery dissolves our bowels. The latrine poles are always densely crowded; the people at home ought to be shown these grey, yellow, miserable, wasted faces here, these bent figures from whose bodies the colic wrings out the blood, and who with lips trembling and distorted with pain, grin at one another and say:

"It is not much sense pulling up one's trousers again —"

Our artillery is fired out, it has too few shells and the barrels are so worn that they shoot uncertainly, and scatter so widely as even to fall on ourselves. We have too few horses. Our fresh troops are anaemic boys in need of rest, who cannot carry a pack, but merely know how to die. By thousands. They understand nothing about warfare, they simply go on and let themselves be shot down. A single flyer routed two companies of them for a joke, just as they came fresh from the train—before they had ever heard of such a thing as cover.

"Germany ought to be empty soon," says Kat.

We have given up hope that some day an end may come. We never think so far. A man can stop a bullet and be killed; he can get wounded, and then the hospital is his next stop. There, if they do not amputate him, he sooner or later falls into the hands of one of those staff surgeons who, with the War Service Cross in his button-hole, says to him: "What, one leg a bit short? If you have any pluck you don't need to run at the front. The man is A1. Dismiss!"

Kat tells a story that has travelled the whole length of the front from the Vosges to Flanders;—of the staff surgeon who reads the names on the list, and when a man comes before him, without looking up, says: "A1. We need soldiers up there." A fellow with a wooden leg comes up before him, the staff surgeon again says A1—"And then," Kat raises his voice, "the fellow says to him: 'I already have a wooden leg, but when I go back again and they shoot off my head, then I will get a wooden head made and become a staff surgeon.'" This answer tickles us all immensely.

There may be good doctors, and there are, lots of them; all the same, every soldier some time during his hundreds of inspections falls into the clutches of one of these countless hero-grabbers who pride themselves on changing as many C3's and B3's as possible into A1's.[1]

There are many such stories, they are mostly far more bitter. All the same, they have nothing to do with mutiny or lead-swinging. They are merely honest and call a thing by its name; for there is a very great deal of fraud, injustice, and baseness in the army. It is nothing that regiment after regiment returns again and again to the ever more hopeless struggle, that attack follows attack along the weakening, retreating, crumbling line.

From a mockery the tanks have become a terrible weapon. Armoured they come rolling on in long lines, more than anything else embody for us the horror of war.

We do not see the guns that bombard us; the attacking lines of the enemy infantry are men like ourselves; but these tanks are machines, their caterpillars run on as endless as the war, they are annihilation, they roll without feeling into the craters, and climb up again without stopping, a fleet of roaring, smoke-belching armour-clads, invulnerable steel beasts squashing the dead and the wounded—we shrivel up in our thin skin before them, against their colossal weight our arms are sticks of straw, and our hand-grenades matches.

Shells, gas clouds, and flotillas of tanks—shattering, corroding, death.

Dysentery, influenza, typhus—scalding, choking, death.

Trenches, hospitals, the common grave—there are no other possibilities.

* * *

It is autumn. There are not many of the old hands left. I am the last of the seven fellows from our class.

Everyone talks of peace and armistice. All wait. If it again proves an illusion, then they will break up; hope is high, it cannot be taken away again without an upheaval. If there is not peace, then there will be revolution.

---

[1] For the translation into English, the categories for types of military service are given in their official British equivalent for its recruits: A1 meant fit for military service in every way; B3 meant suitable for sedentary work abroad; and C3 (the lowest classification) designated someone fit only for sedentary service at home.

I have fourteen days rest, because I have swallowed a bit of gas; in the little garden I sit the whole day long in the sun. The armistice is coming soon, I believe it now too. Then we will go home.

Here my thoughts stop and will not go any farther. All that meets me, all that floods over me are but feelings—greed of life, love of home, yearning for the blood, intoxication of deliverance. But no aims.

Had we returned home in 1916, out of the suffering and the strength of our experience we might have unleashed a storm. Now if we go back we will be weary, broken, burnt out, rootless, and without hope. We will not be able to find our way any more.

And men will not understand us—for the generation that grew up before us, though it has passed these years with us already had a home and a calling; now it will return to its old occupations, and the war will be forgotten—and the generation that has grown up after us will be strange to us and push us aside. We will be superfluous even to ourselves, we will grow older, a few will adapt themselves, some others will merely submit, and most will be bewildered;—the years will pass by and in the end we shall fall into ruin.

But perhaps all this that I think is mere melancholy and dismay, which will fly away as the dust, when I stand once again beneath the poplars and listen to the rustling of their leaves. It cannot be that it has gone, the yearning that made our blood unquiet, the unknown, the perplexing, the oncoming things, the thousand faces of the future, the melodies from dreams and from books, the whispers and divinations of women; it cannot be that this has vanished in bombardment, in despair, in brothels.

Here the trees show gay and golden, the berries of the rowan stand red among the leaves, country roads run white out to the sky line, and the canteens hum like beehives with rumours of peace.

I stand up.

I am very quiet. Let the months and years come, they can take nothing from me, they can take nothing more. I am so alone, and so without hope that I can confront them without fear. The life that has borne me through these years is still in my hands and my eyes. Whether I have subdued it, I know not. But so long as it is there it will seek its own way out, heedless of the will that is within me.

52

HELEN ZENNA SMITH

Not So Quiet . . .

1930

Two years after the publication of All Quiet on the Western Front *(Document 51), a feminist response appeared. It is a testament to the power and popularity of Erich Maria Remarque's novel that it could provide a precise framework for the later novel published by the Australian-born popular novelist Evadne Price under the pseudonym Helen Zenna Smith (1896/1901–1985). Although not directly autobiographical,* Not So Quiet . . . *provides a narration of the war from the firsthand perspective of a young woman who drives an ambulance along the western front. This novel is very much a product of its time, offering a feminist antiwar message that controversially and at times melodramatically places the sufferings of noncombatants close to the war zone at the forefront. Like* All Quiet on the Western Front, *it illustrates the war generation's attitude toward authority, its skepticism about heroism, and its appreciation of war's futility and waste—emotions and experiences that transcended not only national boundaries but in some cases even the divide between combatants and noncombatants, and between men and women.*

"Hark!" interrupts Misery. "Hark!"

The enemy planes have come within earshot. Buzz, buzz, buzz . . . like a giant hive of giant bees.

"Bigger fleet than ever to-night."

The gossip and the laughter die down to a murmur, then gradually fade away altogether. We sit there in the semi-darkness waiting. It is not the most pleasant sensation in the world sitting in a shelter waiting for bombs to drop. Even though the odds are a hundred to one against a direct hit, it is a nasty feeling . . . like anticipating a dentist's drill, or making a speech in public, or hearing a burglar trying an insecure window-catch . . . apprehensive, uncertain what may happen next.

Now the picnic has started. The bombs are falling thick and fast, each explosion nearer. Worse to-night than they have ever been, we whisper.

From Helen Zenna Smith, *Not So Quiet* . . . (London: A. E. Marriot, 1930), 234–39.

We whisper the same thing every night. In the half-light I can see Misery's fingers working rapidly . . . in and out she wriggles the crochet hook, her voice murmuring . . . "Two chain, three treble, two double crochet, four treble, turn, two chain. . . ." Her plain, gaunt, absorbed face bends over the work as though she can see the pattern plainly. She has been working on the bedspread for eighteen months . . . another six months and it will be ready for her and Fred. "*If* the war ends then, but wot 'ope?" says Misery, always the perfect pessimist.

There is a terrific explosion, startling in its unexpectedness, like a frightful peal of thunder, followed by a rain of shots. We know what that is . . . machine guns aimed from the air at some target after the bomb has scored a hit. We sit up. Hardly have we recovered from the shock than there is another ear-splitting explosion . . . nearer. More machine-gun fire follows it. Now we see the machines overhead, outlined black against the clear sky. The bombs are dropping all round the trench. Our ears are ringing. We are all deathly quiet now, watching . . . all but Misery, who crochets for dear life. Another bomb and another hail of machine-gun fire. We stare at one another, not daring to ask what we are all thinking. . . .

Ploo-oop. Crash! Through the half-light our eyes seek one another, startled. We listen. Four engines. We can count them distinctly. Four bombers flying low over our trench. Someone asks what our own planes are doing to let the raiders through like this, dropping their bombs like rain, deafening us until our heads are pounding and our ear-drums throbbing.

"Put that blarsted crochay away," whispers Blimey harshly. "Fair get on my nerves you do, crochayin' as though they was playin' marbles up there with them bombs; gettin' on everybody's nerves you are with yer rotten crochay. . . ."

Ploo-op. Crash!

The end of the trench suddenly collapses with a roar. There is a flash of flame outside. The sandbags cave in slowly as though coming to a mighty decision before falling. The bomb has caught the end of the trench. Five feet to the left and the airman would have scored a direct hit. One of the girls is hit—bleeding. The others begin to panic and huddle together at the other end. The plane comes down in a swoop, lower, lower . . . engine roaring. We can see his bombs hanging below the wings. Lower, lower . . . another bomb is unleashed. It falls in the middle of the trench. There is a mighty explosion, a flash of flame, an ear-splitting percussion that knocks me flat on the ground. Something falls on me. I lose consciousness. When I come to girls are screaming all round me . . . the air is filled with the groans of the dying. Something heavy is lying across my legs. With difficulty I remove it. It is a sandbag. I stand up. My mouth is full of dirt, but I am not hurt. . . .

The trench is like a slaughterhouse. All round me girls are lying dead or dying. Some are wounded. The wounded are trying to staunch one another's blood. A few are shell-shocked. One scales the side of the shelter frantically, scrabbling and digging her toes into the earth like a maddened animal, then runs shrieking into the night. In the distance the buzz of the planes grows fainter and fainter. The raiders have been beaten off at last. . . .

A soldier comes over to where I am sitting on the side of the trench.

"Well, you wasn't meant to die to-night," he says.

I turn my head in his direction and begin to laugh softly. He is alarmed.

"Can't get you a drink, can I? You're not hysterical nor nothing?"

I tell him no. I have never felt less hysterical in my life.

A Chronology of the First World War: From Prelude to Peace (1879–1923)

1879   Dual Alliance of Austria-Hungary and Germany.

1882   Triple Alliance of Italy, Austria-Hungary, and Germany.

1884– 1885   Berlin Conference sets terms for further colonization of Africa by Europe.

1892   Military agreement between France and Russia.

1899   First Hague Conventions signed; start of Boer War (aka South African War).

1902   End of Boer War.

1905   Russo-Japanese War ends in Russian defeat; Revolution in Russia; First Moroccan Crisis.

1907   Second Hague Conventions; Anglo-Russian Entente.

1908   Bosnia-Herzegovina annexed by Austro-Hungarian Empire.

1909   Publication of Futurist manifesto.

1911   Second Moroccan Crisis; Tripoli War.

1912   First Balkan War.

1913   Second Balkan War.

1914   *June 28*   Assassination of Archduke Franz Ferdinand, heir to Austro-Hungarian throne, and his wife, Sophie, in Sarajevo.

July 28   Austria-Hungary declares war on Serbia.

August 1   Germany declares war on Russia.

August 3   Germany declares war on France, sending part of its army through Belgium; Italy declares itself neutral.

August 4   Britain declares war on Germany.

August 6   Austria-Hungary declares war on Russia; Serbia declares war on Germany.

August 10   Britain and France declare war on Austria-Hungary.

August 11   Austria-Hungary invades Serbia.

September 6–12   First Battle of the Marne ends German offensive.

November 1   Russia declares war on Ottoman Empire.

November 5   Other Allies declare war on Ottoman Empire.

1915   *January 7*   First publication of reports of German violations of human rights in occupied France.

January 19   First German zeppelin raid on Britain.

February 2   Start of British naval blockade of Germany.

February 4   Start of German blockade using submarine warfare.

Late February   Protests in Berlin, then London, over increase in cost of living.

April   First use of chemical weapons by Germany on western front.

April 24   Start of attacks on Armenian population in Ottoman Empire.

April 25   British and Australian forces land at Gallipoli.

April 28–May 1   International Congress of Women meets in The Hague.

May   Appearance of Bryce Report, Britain's initial investigation into alleged German atrocities in Belgium.

May 7   Sinking of *Lusitania*, a British ocean liner, by German submarines.

May 19   Creation of British coalition government.

May 23   Italy declares war on Austria-Hungary.

August 4–6   Zeppelin raids on English towns continue.

October 12   Execution of British nurse Edith Cavell for helping Allied soldiers to escape from Belgium.

October 14   Bulgaria joins war against Allied powers.

1916   *January 27*   Britain introduces conscription but excludes Ireland.

January 29–31   German zeppelin raids on Paris and parts of England.

February 21   Start of Battle of Verdun.

April   French civilians in occupied zones are deported for forced labor.

April 24–May 1   Easter Rising in Ireland.

July 1   Start of Battle of the Somme.

August 27   Romania joins Allies.

September 15   Tanks first used by Britain.

October 3   Deportation of Belgians for forced labor begins.

November 27   Greece declares war on Germany.

December 5   Germany's Auxiliary Service Law compels war work by all men ages seventeen to sixty.

December 7   David Lloyd George replaces Herbert Asquith as British prime minister.

1917   *January 23*   Rationing of coal begins in France.

January 31   Germany resumes unrestricted submarine warfare.

February   Demonstrations in Germany protest cost and availability of food.

February 4   Strikes in Petrograd.

March–May   Widespread strikes in France.

March 8   Russian Revolution begins.

March 16   Tsar Nicholas II abdicates.

April   Increased antiwar demonstrations in Germany.

April 6   United States enters the war.

April 16   French offensive along Chemin des Dames begins; mutinies follow.

June 13   Daylight air raids in London do extensive damage.

June 25   First American Expeditionary Forces reach France.

July 31   Third Battle of Ypres (also called Battle of Passchendaele) begins.

August 2   Russia's Provisional Government passes universal adult suffrage.

October 15   Mata Hari, alleged German spy, executed in France.

October 24   Battle of Caporetto begins.

November 7   Second Phase of Russian Revolution gives control of Russia to Bolshevik Party under V. I. Lenin.

November 16   Georges Clemenceau becomes premier of France.

December 15   Armistice between Russia and Germany.

1918   *January*   Strikes by German workers protesting food shortages halt munitions industry; similar strikes occur in Vienna and Budapest.

February 6   British Parliament passes Representation of the People Act enfranchising some British women for first time.

March 3   Treaty of Brest-Litovsk cedes Russian imperial territory to Germany and formally takes Russia out of the war.

March 21   German offensive along the Somme begins.

March 23   Long-range German cannons bombard Paris.

April 2   First American troops engage in battle on western front.

July 15   Second Battle of the Marne begins.

September 29   Bulgaria signs armistice with Allies.

October 29   German naval mutiny begins at Kiel.

October 30   Ottoman Empire signs armistice with Allies.

November 3   Austria-Hungary signs armistice with Allies.

November 8   Insurrection in Munich; workers declare a republic.

November 9   Abdication of Kaiser Wilhelm II; Social Democrats assume control of Germany amid strikes and unrest.

November 11   Germany signs armistice with Allies.

December   Demobilization of British army begins.

1919   *January 15*   Murder of German revolutionary leaders Rosa Luxemburg and Karl Liebknecht.

January 18   Paris Peace Conference begins.

June 28   Treaty of Versailles signed.

July 12   Blockade of Germany ends.

November 19   U.S. Senate rejects Treaty of Versailles.

1920   *August 10*   Treaty of Sèvres, formal peace between Allied states and Ottoman Turkey, rejected by Turkish nationalists.

November 11   Unveiling of Tomb of the Unknown Warrior in London and Tomb of the Unknown Soldier in Paris.

1921   *August*   Treaty of Berlin signed, officially ending war between United States and Germany.

November 4   Dedication of Tomb of the Unknown Soldier in Rome.

1923   *July 24*   Final peace treaty of the war, Treaty of Lausanne, signed between newly established Turkey and most major Allied powers.

Questions for Consideration

1. What factors motivated the creation of alliances (Document 1) between European powers in the decades before the First World War began? What cultural, political, or social factors worked to limit such ties (Documents 2–5)?

2. How important were nationalism and imperialism—the possession and maintenance of colonies—for various European powers prior to the outbreak of the war? In what ways did these forces shape the experience of the war (Documents 6, 17, and 18)? What effects did the war have on European nationalism (Document 50)? On imperialism (Documents 44 and 48)?

3. Participant nations had, to at least some extent, literate populations. How did the literature that emerged from this war shape the ways in which the war experience was conveyed, imagined, and ultimately remembered (Documents 7, 8, 21, 29, 31, 39, 40, 51, and 52)? How did visual propaganda and music—cultural artifacts that did not necessarily rely on literacy—disperse messages about the war's purpose and costs (Documents 9–12 and 26)?

4. The Hague Conventions (Document 2) tried to restrict the use of certain kinds of weapons and attacks and to safeguard prisoners of war. Based on the firsthand accounts presented here, how effective were such restrictions in preventing abuses and shaping the expectations of those involved in the war (Documents 13–19)?

5. The documents offer firsthand perspectives from both combatants and noncombatants and from women as well as men. How connected were the experiences of these different witnesses (Documents 13–21, 29, 30, 32–34, and especially Document 23)? When and how did gender matter?

6. How did those serving in the military see one another across enemy lines (Documents 13–15)? Were there common experiences that transcended national differences? Explain. To what extent did national experiences prove unique? How did the presence of colonial troops affect the relationships between men serving in the military (Documents 16–18, and 48)?

7. From the outbreak of the war, prominent intellectuals sought to make sense of the changes and devastation it wrought. How did the new field of psychology contribute to this process (Documents 36–38)? What light do the more general conclusions of Sigmund Freud (Document 36) and Gustave Le Bon (Document 37) shed on the documents detailing personal experiences of the war?

8. There was certainly widespread support for the war, at least at the outset, but there was also opposition. What were some of the most significant factors motivating opposition to the war (Documents 3, 4, 8, and 28)? How did various governments respond? What role, for example, did the scarcity of food and other resources play in contributing to dissent (Documents 27 and 34)? How did opposition to the war evolve into more revolutionary demands for a new society and a new polity (Document 35)?

9. To what extent do the terms of the Treaty of Versailles (Document 43) reflect efforts to prevent the First World War from occurring again? To what extent can they be seen as trying to make sense of the war's losses? To what extent are they efforts to shape a new global order, including an imperial one?

10. One of the war's legacies was the creation of new states in what became known as the Middle East. How did the diplomatic arrangements that led to this territorial reconfiguration reflect the interests of European states (Documents 45 and 46)? How did the failure of the Austro-Hungarian, German, Ottoman, and Russian empires at war's end help reshape the postwar world in this region and elsewhere?

11. What does postwar culture—either in the realm of art or war literature—reveal about the varying legacies of the war (Documents 49 and 51)? Were these legacies substantially different for people in different states, civilians and combatants, and men and women? If so, in what ways?

Selected Bibliography

GENERAL WORKS: OVERVIEWS, ANALYSIS, AND ANTHOLOGIES

Audoin-Rouzeau, Stéphane, and Annette Becker. *14–18: Understanding the Great War.* Translated by Catherine Temerson. New York: Hill & Wang, 2002.

Beckett, Ian F. W. *The Great War, 1914–1918.* Harlow, U.K.: Longman, 2001.

Coetzee, Frans, and Marilyn Shevin-Coetzee, eds. *Authority, Identity, and the Social History of the Great War.* Providence, R.I.: Berghahn, 1995.

De Groot, Gerard J. *The First World War.* Basingstoke, U.K.: Palgrave, 2001.

Eksteins, Modris. *The Rites of Spring: The Great War and the Birth of the Modern Age.* Boston: Houghton Mifflin, 1989.

Ellis, John, and Michael Cox. *The World War I Databook.* London: Aurum Press, 2001.

Fussell, Paul. *The Great War and Modern Memory.* Oxford, U.K.: Oxford University Press, 1975.

Grayzel, Susan R. *Women and the First World War.* Harlow, U.K.: Longman, 2002.

Hannah, James, ed. *The Great War Reader.* College Station: Texas A&M University Press, 2000.

Higonnet, Margaret R., ed. *Lines of Fire: Women Writers of World War I.* New York: Plume, 1999.

Keegan, John. *The First World War.* New York: Knopf, 2000.

Kitchen, Martin. *Europe between the Wars.* Harlow, U.K.: Longman, 1988.

Kramer, Alan. *Dynamic of Destruction: Culture and Mass Killing in the First World War.* Oxford, U.K.: Oxford University Press, 2007.

Morrow, John H., Jr. *The Great War: An Imperial History.* London: Routledge, 2005.

Neiberg, Michael S. *Fighting the Great War: A Global History.* Cambridge, Mass.: Harvard University Press, 2005.

Palmer, Svetlana, and Sarah Wallis, eds. *Intimate Voices from the First World War.* New York: HarperCollins, 2003.

Strachan, Hew. *The First World War.* Vol. 1, *To Arms.* Oxford, U.K.: Oxford University Press, 2001.

———, ed. *World War I: A History*. Oxford, U.K.: Oxford University Press, 1998.

Vansittart, Peter. *Voices from the Great War*. New York: Watt, 1984.

Winter, Jay, and Blaine Baggett. *The Great War and the Shaping of the Twentieth Century*. New York: Penguin, 1996.

BATTLE ZONES

Horne, John, and Alan Kramer. *German Atrocities, 1914: A History of Denial*. New Haven, Conn.: Yale University Press, 2001.

Howard, Michael, George J. Andreopoulos, and Mark R. Shulman, eds. *The Laws of War: Constraints on Warfare in the Western World*. New Haven, Conn.: Yale University Press, 1994.

Liulevicius, Vejas Gabriel. *War Land on the Eastern Front: Culture, National Identity and German Occupation in World War I*. Cambridge, U.K.: Cambridge University Press, 2000.

Lunn, Joe. *Memoirs of the Maelstrom: A Senegalese Oral History of the First World War*. Portsmouth, N.H.: Heinemann, 1999.

Kennett, Lee. *The First Air War, 1914–1918*. New York: Free Press, 1991.

Kramer, Alan. *Dynamic of Destruction: Culture and Mass Killing in the First World War*. Oxford, U.K.: Oxford University Press, 2007.

Page, Melvin, ed. *Africa and the First World War*. New York: St. Martin's, 1987.

Rachamimov, Alon. *POWs and the Great War: Captivity on the Eastern Front*. Oxford, U.K.: Berg, 2002.

Roper, Michael. *The Secret Battle: Emotional Survival in the Great War*. Manchester, U.K.: Manchester University Press, 2009.

Smith, Leonard V. *Between Mutiny and Obedience*. Princeton, N.J.: Princeton University Press, 1994.

Strachan, Hew. *The First World War*. Harmondsworth, U.K.: Penguin, 2003.

Thompson, Mark, *The White War: Life and Death on the Italian Front*. New York: Basic Books, 2008.

THE WAR AT HOME: SOCIETY, CULTURE, AND POLITICS

Condell, Diana, and Jean Liddiard. *Working for Victory? Images of Women in the First World War, 1914–1918*. London: Routledge, 1987.

Daniel, Ute. *The War from Within: German Working-Class Women in the First World War*. Oxford, U.K.: Berg, 1997.

Davis, Belinda. *Home Fires Burning: Food, Politics, and Everyday Life in World War I Berlin*. Chapel Hill: University of North Carolina Press, 2000.

Downs, Laura Lee. *Manufacturing Inequality: Gender Division in the French and British Metalworking Industries, 1914–1939*. Ithaca, N.Y.: Cornell University Press, 1995.

Fridenson, Patrick, ed. *The French Home Front, 1914–1918*. Oxford, U.K.: Berg, 1992.

Gatrell, Peter. *A Whole Empire Walking: Refugees in Russia during World War I.* Bloomington: University of Indiana Press, 2005.

Gregory, Adrian. *The Last Great War: British Society and the First World War.* Cambridge, U.K.: Cambridge University Press, 2008.

Gullace, Nicoletta F. *"The Blood of Our Sons": Men, Women, and the Renegotiation of British Citizenship during the Great War.* New York: Palgrave Macmillan, 2002.

Hanna, Martha, ed. and trans. *Your Death Would Be Mine: Paul and Marie Pireaud in the Great War.* Cambridge, Mass.: Harvard University Press, 2006.

Healy, Maureen. *Vienna and the Fall of the Habsburg Empire: Total War and Everyday Life in World War I.* Cambridge, U.K.: Cambridge University Press, 2004.

Higonnet, Margaret R., et al., eds. *Behind the Lines: Gender and the Two World Wars.* New Haven, Conn.: Yale University Press, 1987.

Horne, John, *Labour at War: France and Britain 1914–1918.* Oxford, U.K.: Clarendon Press, 1991.

———, ed. *State, Society and Mobilization in Europe during the First World War.* Cambridge, U.K.: Cambridge University Press, 1997.

Jahn, Hubertus F. *Patriotic Culture in Russia during World War I.* Ithaca, N.Y.: Cornell University Press, 1995.

Melman, Billie, ed. *Borderlines: Genders and Identities in War and Peace, 1870–1930.* New York: Routledge, 1998.

Paret, Peter, Beth Irwin Lewis, and Paul Paret. *Persuasive Images: Posters of War and Revolution from the Hoover Institution Archives.* Princeton, N.J.: Princeton University Press, 1992.

Pedersen, Susan. *Family, Dependence, and the Origins of the Welfare State: Britain and France, 1914–1945.* Cambridge, U.K.: Cambridge University Press, 1993.

Robb, George. *British Culture and the First World War.* Harlow, U.K.: Longman, 2002.

Roshwald, Aviel, and Richard Stites, eds. *European Culture in the Great War: The Arts, Entertainment, and Propaganda, 1914–1918.* Cambridge, U.K.: Cambridge University Press, 1999.

Sweeney, Regina M. *Singing Our Way to Victory: French Cultural Politics and Music during the Great War.* Middletown, Conn.: Wesleyan University Press, 2001.

Thom, Deborah. *Nice Girls and Rude Girls: Women Workers in World War I.* London: I. B. Tauris, 1998.

Verhey, Jeffrey. *The Spirit of 1914: Militarism, Myth and Mobilization in Germany.* Cambridge, U.K.: Cambridge University Press, 2000.

Wall, Richard, and Jay Winter, eds. *The Upheaval of War: Family, Work and Welfare in Europe, 1914–1918.* Cambridge, U.K.: Cambridge University Press, 1988.

Winter, Jay, and Jean-Louis Robert, eds. *Capital Cities at War: London, Paris, Berlin, 1914–1919.* Vols. 1 and 2. Cambridge, U.K.: Cambridge University Press, 1997, 2007.

ORIGINS AND LEGACIES

Brubaker, Rogers. *Citizenship and Nationhood in France and Germany.* Cambridge, Mass.: Harvard University Press, 1992.

Cohen, Deborah. *The War Come Home: Disabled Veterans in Britain and Germany, 1914–1939.* Berkeley and Los Angeles: University of California Press, 2001.

Fischer, Fritz. *Germany's Aims in the First World War.* New York: W. W. Norton, 1967.

Fromkin, David. *A Peace to End All Peace: The Fall of the Ottoman Empire and the Creation of the Modern Middle East.* New York: Henry Holt, 1989.

Goldstein, Erik. *The First World War Peace Settlements, 1919–1925.* Harlow, U.K.: Longman, 2002.

Hull, Isabel V. *Absolute Destruction: Military Culture and the Practices of War in Imperial Germany.* Ithaca, N.Y.: Cornell University Press, 2005.

Joll, James. *The Origins of the First World War.* London: Longman, 1984.

MacMillan, Margaret. *Paris 1919: Six Months That Changed the World.* New York: Random House, 2001.

Mosse, George L. *Fallen Soldiers: Reshaping the Memory of the World Wars.* New York: Oxford University Press, 1990.

Sherman, Daniel J. *The Construction of Memory in Interwar France.* Chicago: University of Chicago Press, 1999.

Williamson, Samuel R., Jr., and Russel Van Wyk. *July 1914: Soldiers, Statesmen, and the Coming of the Great War: A Brief Documentary History.* Boston: Bedford/St. Martin's, 2003.

Winter, Jay. *Sites of Memory, Sites of Mourning: The Great War in European Cultural History.* Cambridge, U.K.: Cambridge University Press, 1995.

Acknowledgments (continued from p. iv)

Document 5. "Manifesto of Futurism" from *Marinetti: Selected Writings by F. T. Marinetti*, edited by R. W. Flint, translated by R. W. Flint and Arthur A. Coppotelli. Translation copyright © 1972 by Farrar, Straus and Giroux, LLC. Reprinted by permission of Farrar, Straus and Giroux, LLC.

Document 8. Anna Akhmatova, "July 1914" from *The White Flock (Bella Staya) 1917*, translated by John Henriksen. Used by permission of John Henriksen.

Document 9. Imperial War Museum Image Number IWM PST 2763. Copyright © Imperial War Museum.

Document 10. Bundesarchiv, Plak 001-005-070 / Fritz Erler. Courtesy of the Political Poster Collection, GE 364, Hoover Institution Archives.

Document 11. Imperial War Museum Image Number IWM PST 4335. Copyright © Imperial War Museum. Courtesy of the Political Poster Collection, RU/SU 1225, Hoover Institution Archives.

Document 12. Imperial War Museum Image Number IWM PST 2713. Copyright © Imperial War Museum. Courtesy of the Political Poster Collection, FR 670, Hoover Institution Archives.

Documents 17 and 18. From David Omissi, *Indian Voices of the Great War: Soldiers' Letters, 1914–1918*. Selected and introduced by David Omissi, St. Martin's Press, 1999.

Document 19. From Mehmen Arif Ölçen, *Vetluga Memoir: A Turkish Prisoner of War in Russia, 1916–1918*, translated and edited by Gary Leiser. Copyright © 1995 by The Board of Regents of the State of Florida. Reprinted with permission of the University Press of Florida.

Document 20. From Lidiia Zakharova, "Diary of a Red Cross Sister in the Front Lines," translated by Cynthia Simmons and printed in *Lines of Fire: Women Writers of World War I*, edited by Margaret R. Higonnet (New York: Plume, 1999). Used by permission of Cynthia Simmons.

Document 21. From Henri Barbusse, *Under Fire*, translated by Robin Buss (Penguin Classics 2003). Translation copyright © Robin Buss, 2003. Introduction copyright © Jay Winter, 2003. Reproduced by permission of Penguin Books, Ltd.

Document 22. From *The Diary of Gino Speranza: Italy, 1915–1919* Volume II: 1917–1919, edited by Florence Colgate Speranza. Copyright © 1941 by Columbia University Press. Reprinted by permission of the publisher.

Document 23. Reprinted by permission of the publisher from *Your Death Would Be Mine: Paul and Marie Pireaud in the Great War* by Martha Hann, pp. 26, 78. Cambridge, Mass.: Harvard University Press. Copyright © 2006 by Martha Hanna. Translation by the author.

Document 27. Brandenburgisches Landeshauptarchiv, Potsdam, Provinz Brandenburg, Repositur 30, Berlin C, Titel 95, Polizeipräsidium, Nrs. 15809, 15814, 15821, 15851. Contributed, translated, and introduced by Belinda Davis in *Lives and Voices: Sources in European Women's History*, edited by Lisa Di Caprio and Merry E. Wiesner (Wadsworth Publishing, 2000). Used by permission.

Document 29. From *Lines of Fire: Women Writers of World War I*, edited by Margaret R. Higonnet (Plume, 1999). Used by permission of Sanford J. Greenburger Associates, Inc.

Document 30. *Deutsche Frauen, Deustche Treue 1814–1933* (German Women, German and Loyal [True]), published in 1935. Reprinted in *The Virago Book of Women and the Great War*, edited by Joyce Marlow (London: Virago, 1998). Used by permission.

Index

Addams, Jane, 95
aeronautics, innovations in, 19. *See also* aircraft; air raids
Africa
colonial troops from, 5, 22–24, 52–53
European colonization of, 161
imperial struggles over, 4
war in, 24
Agadir, Germany and, 7
aggression, Freud on, 114–16
aircraft, 19
Wells on, 47–49
air raids, 19–20, 162
daylight, in London, 163
Akhmatova, Anna (Anna Andreyevna Gorenko), "July 1914," 2, 55
Albania, creation of, 8
alliances and alliance system, 5–6. *See also specific alliances*
multinational, 5–6
in 1914, 9
origins of war and, 41–42
Ottomans in, 6–7
Allies
declaration of war on Ottoman Empire, 162
fronts opened by, 15
Italy on, 15
Japan and, 24
naval blockade by, 19, 162
postwar occupations by, 31, 138–39
Romania in, 162
troop composition for, 24
"All Quiet on the Western Front" (Remarque), 33–34, 153–57
Alsace, France, and, 29
America. *See* United States
"America First, Now and Hereafter" (*Chicago Daily Tribune*), 130
American Expeditionary Forces, 163
ammunition, 13
Anglo-French Entente, 6
Anglo-Russian Entente, 6, 41, 161

Anglo-Saxon races, 5
annexations, by Austria-Hungary, 6, 161
anti-Semitism, 5. *See also* Jews
antiwar sentiment, 13–15, 27
in "All Quiet on the Western Front" (Remarque), 153–57
in Germany, 163
in literature, 46
"April Theses" (Lenin), 27, 109–13
armed forces. *See also* military; navy; soldiers
German, 28
nationalist, 3
Armenians, Ottoman massacres of, 15–17, 87–89, 162
armistice
Russian-German, 163
signings in 1918, 164
soldiers and battles after, 29
war ended by (1918), 28–29
Arras, battle at, 15
artillery, 12
arts. *See also* poetry; *specific works*
postwar, 33–34
Asia. *See also* Japan
imperial struggles over, 4
war in, 24
Asquith, Herbert, 20
assassination, of Franz Ferdinand, 10, 161
Australia
Pacific mandates of, 32
troops from, 24
women's voting rights in, 33
Austria. *See also* Austria-Hungary
autonomy of, 31
and battle of Caporetto, 27
peace treaty with, 133
Prussian defeat of, 4
women's voting rights in, 33
Austria-Hungary. *See also* Austria
annexation of Bosnia-Herzegovina by, 6, 161
armistice in, 164

173